THE
DO-IT-YOURSELF
BAILOUT

TESTIMONIALS

"Hey Ken, I bought your book almost a year ago, followed it step by step and settled on one incoming phone call, two credit cards totaling $55,000 for $10,000. I refer you to all my friends in need. It really works!! Thanks A Million$" — Sam X. Torrance, Calif.

"I had $235,000 in credit card debt. I was one week away from filing Chapter 7 bankruptcy when I ordered *The Do-It-Yourself Bailout*. This book inspired me and gave me the guidance to negotiate these balances down to close to $40,000, about 15% of what I originally owed. Thanks Kenny." — Steve, Roundhill, Va.

"Thanks to the encouragement and information in your book I've recently settled $54,000 of debt for $15,000." — Mark D., Los Angeles, Calif.

"I bought your book and have been following it to the letter (!) with two credit cards that I'm unable to pay due to a 40% pay cut. The first one just settled with me today for $8,700 on a $21,000 debt. Whew. Thank you so much for that." — S. B. New York

"I really found your book helpful! I am now in a very empowered state most of the time with everything, but I was super-stressed out for a long time!" — Chuck B., Phoenix, Ariz.

"I just wanted to thank you for your useful information in this book. I will recommend it to a lot of friends." — Marc D., Los Angeles, Calif.

"My income has drastically reduced in the past two years, and my debt has gone through the roof. I have started reading your book, It is exactly what I have been searching for." — Mark E.

All testimonials are excerpts from emails received from actual readers. While there are many readers I have not heard from, and I'm sure many who have not achieved this type of outcome, if any, the results indicated in these testimonials were achieved by "average" people (the Federal Trade Commission's term, not mine, I consider all my readers to be exceptional) who reduced their debt on his own after reading The Do-It-Yourself Bailout. *No one received any compensation in cash or trade for their testimonial. Kenny Golde*

THE DO-IT-YOURSELF BAILOUT

How I Eliminated $222,000 of Credit-Card Debt in Eighteen Months and Saved Nearly $150,000.

KENNY GOLDE

Published by Barricade Books Inc.
2037 Lemoine Ave.
Suite 362
Fort Lee, NJ 07024
www.barricadebooks.com

Library of Congress Cataloging-in-Publication Data

Golde, Kenny.
The do-it-yourself bailout : how I eliminated $222,000 of
credit-card debt in eighteen months and saved nearly $150,000 /
Kenny Golde.
    p. cm.
ISBN: 978-1-56980-473-5
1. Credit cards. 2. Consumer credit. 3. Debt. 4. Finance,
Personal. I. Title.
HG3755.G65 2013
332.7'65--dc23
                                                            2012037328
          ISBN: 978-1-56980-473-5

    10 9 8 7 6 5 4 3 2 1

Manufactured in the United States of America

ACKNOWLEDGEMENTS

This book would not have been clear, concise, or grammatically correct without the patient assistance of my mother, Judy. I want to thank all the friends who took me to lunch and patiently listened to my "story" without bludgeoning me. I want to thank everyone who contributed to my going into debt, for the journey has been valuable. I want to thank the two men who very directly made this journey possible, Lawrence Gabriel and Mark Gabriel. And I want to thank everyone who contributed to the process of my understanding of how to take the journey: Mark Safran, Bob Golde, Sandy Stotzer, Jim Crawford, Alon Ben-Nun, Dan Smith, Mark Elkins, Shane Curtis, Robert Goodman, Bry Sanders, Larry Ecoff, Jonathan Aluzas, Steve Bryson, Gary Weiss, John Somerville, Pedro Tapia, John Donaldson, David Crawford, Fred Cei, Scott Coady and the Institute for Embodied Wisdown, Peggy Biocini, Mark Bass, Matt Tapie, Gary Schein, O.T. Vickers, Andy Reich, Jeff Hare, Jodi Davis, Jodi Womack, Steve and Suzanne Roy, David Golde, Gabriella Zielinksi, Jonathan Klein, Zen de Brucke, Kathleen Coady, Lindsey Welch, Giselle Fernandez, Napoloeon Hill, Landmark Education, Blood Soldiers, C.J., and my love, Marshell.

DISCLAIMER

I am not an attorney, and nothing in this book is meant to be advice, legal or otherwise. This book represents only my experiences and my interpretation of information that I have gained through those experiences. Every situation is different, and laws vary from state to state. I make no recommendation that you should proceed with debt settlement negotiations in a manner similar to or based on my experiences as related herein, nor do I make any warranty, express or implied, that you will have experiences or results similar to or even related to mine. Please visit an attorney and an accountant with expertise in the area of debt settlement and/or bankruptcy to discuss your personal situation and how anything you read in this book may, or may not, apply to it.

TABLE OF CONTENTS

INTRODUCTION

My name is Kenny Golde. I am a real person.

In 2005, I had just bought my first home, a duplex in Los Angeles, near Hollywood. I had less than $10,000 in credit-card debt, more than $100,000 in unused lines of credit, a FICO score of more than 800, and about $100,000 in savings even after the down payment on my home. At thirty-eight-years old, I felt that I had taken a great step into my future and was looking forward to finding a soul mate and starting a family as my career progressed. I even adopted a dog.

Over the next two years, I would see my financial situation be entirely reversed. Even before the financial crisis of 2008 had hit the world, a few unexpected turns in my business would cause my savings to fall to less than $50,000 and my credit-card debt to swell to more than $200,000. My monthly minimum payments on credit cards alone totaled nearly $3,600. By late 2007, I estimated that I had five months to go before being completely destitute, losing my home and going bankrupt.

Not where I expected to be at forty. Not by a million dollars.

After I had accumulated my debt, I began to research my options. I found many books and websites on debt reduction. An Amazon search for "debt reduction" brought up more than two dozen books. A Google search for "debt reduction" issued pages and pages of websites for books, calculators, programs, consolidators, and opinions on how to reduce debt. Beyond an array of financial-planning tools intended to help people live debt free, or at least debt manageable, as a lifestyle practice, I found that one of the common tools mentioned by many of these debt books, websites, and service resources was the idea that I could call my credit-card companies and negotiate with them to settle my debt for less than I owed.

What I did not find in the books and websites I reviewed was anything more than the simple advice that settling debt was possible. I did not find any book or website that actually took me through the process of approaching my creditors, what to say to them, what to expect them to say to me, how long the process might take, the pitfalls to avoid, or what success I might have. Perhaps something of this nature existed. I did not find it.

Now I have gone through the process. As of this writing, I have reduced my credit-card debt from its cumulative peak of $222,000 to zero. That is correct. I am 100-percent credit-card debt free. I have done this legally, at a fraction of the cost of the debt itself, and I saved just less than $150,000 that was written off entirely! The journey took me about a year and a half. I dealt with six major U.S. banks and acquired a vast, new knowledge of how the process of settling credit-card debt actually works — from the inside.

I do not profess to be an expert in debt or debt reduction, either in concept or reality. I will not state that a particular experience of mine is an absolute, only that it is my experience. I do feel, though, that if you are preparing for the process of settling your own credit-card debt, reading about the experiences of one who has gone before you may be helpful — and not only monetarily.

Carrying debt is about more than money. It is about more than payments or late fees or financial planning. Carrying debt can be an emotional experience. Over the course of my journey, I have felt fear, doubt, shame, failure, incompetence, insecurity, sadness, grief, pain, and anger. At times, through the support of family and friends, I have also felt love, joy, happiness, and fulfillment. In all, it is what my wonderful and caring friend, Jodi, describes as "every emotion, every day." The first step in dealing with my debt was to deal with my emotions, for it became quickly clear that I would not be successful in negotiating with the banks if I allowed fear, doubt, shame, and insecurity to cloud my dealings.

After an extraordinary journey into the complex world of credit, debt, banks, lawsuits, bankruptcy, and global finance, I have emerged with an entirely different relationship to money and personal value.

I've even thought of a new word: Debt-ication, a play on "debt" and "dedication." Their dictionary definitions are:

Dedication: the quality of being dedicated or committed to a task or purpose.

Debt: something, typically money, that is owed or due; and, a feeling of gratitude for a service or favor.

So what is **Debt-ication?**

I am calling it "A feeling of gratitude to the state of owing money. A commitment to the purpose of self-growth through the journey of paying off debts, monetary and personal."

My journey is not unique. Through the last few years of global credit crises, record gas prices, a failing economy, a historic presidential election, massive bank failures, record foreclosures and bankruptcies, I am only one among an immense number of Americans and people from all over the world, of all ages and income levels, who have found that

debt rather than savings is the defining factor of their financial lives. Every one of us has his or her own story of choices,
risks, adventures, hopes, dreams, successes and failures, commitment, passion, crisis, and surprise that has caused us, or
perhaps someone we love, to accumulate debt or anticipate
that we might.

Though I will tell you the story of how I got "into" debt,
it is not the main focus of this book. This book is about
how I got "out." That is what I will share with you, step
by step, month by month, bank by bank, from phone calls
to collection agents to lawsuits to settlement agreements. In
the pages that follow, you will see patterns and events in my
experiences that may cross your path, as well, should you
choose to go the route of debt settlement. If my journey
helps you negotiate your debt with less pain, more confi-
dence, a better attitude, and ultimately, more financial success, then I will be pleased to have shared it.

Chapter 1

MY "STORY"

I WORK IN THE FILM industry as a producer, writer, and director of motion pictures. At the time of the experiences I am going to relate, I was directing an independent film. By "independent," I mean films that are not made at the major Hollywood studios and for the most part, not made with major Hollywood money. The first film I directed cost less than half-a-million dollars to make, and my writing and directing services earned $45,000 over the course of about two years.

For my second film, I had my heart set on a lovely, heartfelt, "make-you-laugh, make-you-cry" drama about a young man whose wife had recently passed away, and his emotional journey to learn that his pain is not unique, to find a way to grieve, and to learn that he still has a beautiful life to live. I had first read the script, *Uncross the Stars*, almost ten years earlier. It was, in Hollywood terminology, a "soft" script, meaning it had no guns, no sex, and no violence.

In 1995, the industry was experiencing the Quentin Tarantino revolution and a series of hip, gangster-related films where colorful bad guys that shoot their pistols sideways were the flavor of the day. Each time I sent out the script for financing, I received the same note: Beautiful script, nothing we can do with it. As the Tarantino phase abated, Hollywood turned to horror films. *Scream* and *The Sixth Sense* re-sparked a worldwide interest in the horror genre, from ghost stories to slasher films. There was simply no room on anyone's slate for a "soft" film about love, loss, and emotional redemption. Always I heard "beautiful script, nothing we can do with it."

Then, in 2004, two movies appeared that changed my future: Zach Braff's hysterically quirky and deeply resonant *Garden State* and Alexander Payne's extraordinary tribute to broken people and California wine, *Sideways*. With the critical and box-office success of these films, a sliver of light fell on the "comedic drama" genre. My film quickly began to generate interest. If this were a book on getting movies made, I'd take you through the details of the five or six deals I had in place for a variety of financing sources, including one out of St. Petersburg, Russia, and how each fell apart for various reasons. But that is another book.

In late 2006, eleven years after first reading *Uncross the Stars*, I succeeded in signing a deal with an investor to finance the film for $560,000. My fee would be $20,000 for another two years' work. At this point, many of you, like my father, will be asking, "Why is he in this business?"

Because I love what I do. I loved this story, and so did my investor, a dear, sweet man named "Gabe." In his late sixties, Gabe was a lovable curmudgeon. He always welcomed me with a smile, a joke, and some complaint about his health. "These g-damn kidney stones feel like a horse is stepping on my balls" was something I can remember him saying.

I learned a valuable lesson from Gabe. For a decade, I had been making films on the basis that they were a good investment for the investors. Budgets, schedules, cash flows, and sales projections were my tools. Working with Gabe, I realized that he was not investing in a film, he was investing in an experience. He was not only trusting me to take care of his money, he was trusting me to *provide* the experience for him. Here was a man who turned seventy the day before I turned forty, bedridden and ill, thanking me for providing him with happiness.

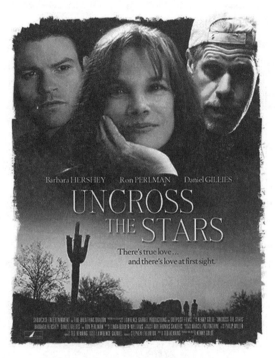

http://www.UncrossTheStarsMovie.com

In April of 2007, I felt as high on life and success as I could imagine. To shoot *Uncross the Stars*, I moved to a little town in Arizona, about twenty miles east of Phoenix, a hot, dry, trailer-speckled town of retirees and scorpions (the real kind, not the Hollywood kind). The townspeople welcomed our film with open arms. The city council, mayor's office, local bank, business owners, and residents loved our script, our crew, and our dollars, and I felt great bringing it all to them.

Although making the film was a lot of fun and creatively satisfying, it quickly became clear that we were underfinanced. I called Gabe in Los Angeles to gain his support in going over budget, only to learn that he had been hospitalized. I decided not to have a financial conversation with him at that time. I didn't want to lay the stress on him. In his condition, he was unable to physically make the calls necessary to procure additional funding. I was faced with the choice of not finishing the picture and waiting for him to recover, then re-mounting the production at a later time, or financing completion myself. I decided to finish the film.

As the shooting progressed and the numbers came in, it added up to about $170,000 over budget. I didn't have $170,000, but I did have that 800 FICO score and several credit cards with wide-open balances. I was able to put about $100,000 on existing cards and take out a new, $75,000 business line of credit to finance completion of photography.

We finished the shoot in late June, and I returned to Los Angeles. I called Gabe to fill him in on the news, but by then, his illness had progressed. He had slipped into a coma, and within a few days, he passed away.

At the funeral, I spoke to one of Gabe's close friends who told me something that would forever make my choice to make this film feel right, despite all the troubles that were still to come. He said that he had spoken with Gabe while we were shooting, before he became so ill, and that Gabe told him making this movie was the last, great experience of his life.

With Gabe gone, I found myself carrying both grief and debt simultaneously. It was a draining and debilitating predicament, similar, I am sure, to the individual stories that many people have. The accumulation of debt, especially large personal debt, is often accompanied by a personal story of loss, tragedy, or surprise that leaves us with both financial and emotional worries, concurrently.

I forced myself to move forward into post-production, continuing to finance another $70,000 in expenses on the film, bringing my total contribution to $240,000. I maxed out my credit lines at $212,000 and had to spend the remaining nearly $30,000 in cash, a crushing blow to my savings account, which was dwindling fast. I was carrying around $3,600 per month in minimum credit-card payments in addition to my mortgage and regular monthly expenses. My total monthly output was nearly $8,000. I estimated that I had about six months of carrying this level of expense with no income before I was destitute.

Why did I have no income? Well, first, I was still working full time on the film to finish it. A job that would earn a few thousand a month would only draw things out and do little more than service the credit-card interest. I couldn't foresee a job that would cover my full $8,000 in monthly expenses, which meant even with a job I'd still be in negative cash flow.

Additionally, at this time, the Writers Guild of America was in the middle of a strike, and the Screen Actors Guild was preparing for one. So the job market in the film industry was tighter than usual. I made the choice to focus my time on finishing and selling the film. That seemed to be the best way to raise several hundred thousand dollars quickly to pay off my debts and be liquid again.

Unfortunately, as credit tightened in late 2007 and 2008, so did the acquisition slates of film distributors. As months passed, it seemed that a sale would take much longer than I had thought. I worried that my cash-flow rate would eliminate my savings before I sold the film.

My next thought was to sell my home. My mortgage was $665,000. In the summer of 2007, when I was shooting the film, I toyed with the (unrealistic) notion of selling for $799,000. After commissions and closing costs I might have netted $740,000, which would have left me $75,000 to put down against what I owed on my credit cards. How many of you have toiled over numbers such as these? Purchase price, sales price (always hopefully high), commissions, closing costs? Any of you have back taxes? I was up to $14,000 in unpaid homeowner's taxes. By November 2007, when I did list the house at $799,000, any boat in that neighborhood had long since sailed. I dropped the listing to $775,000 and then $750,000, and when it expired in May 2008, I hadn't had a single offer. Not even a single looker. By this time, the housing market was in its sharp decline. Fannie Mae and Freddie Mac were tanking, and I expected that the house wouldn't even fetch what I owed. It obviously wouldn't help my debt situation to sell a house that would net me no income.

I was scared.

Sound familiar? Perhaps, if you live in Los Angeles and work in the film industry, my story sounds just like yours. But the details do not matter. The plight of writers and actors in Hollywood may be of no importance to you if you work in the retail industry, or airlines, or real estate, or banking. If you own a small business, work on commission, or collect a salary, the financial crisis of the past few years has hit you, and if you are reading this, the details of how I accumulated my debt may not be of particular interest to you, but how I have resolved much of that debt will be.

If your home or your investments have tumbled in value, or you have taken out new lines of credit to shore up your business in a failing economy, you may share my fear. If you have begun using credit cards not as sources of interim financing to make purchasing easier or as short-term loans for one-time, exceptional expenses like a vacation, but as the means to live month to month, making up the gap between income and basic expenses, then you will identify with my dilemma.

Beyond my fear, I felt like a failure. I had been raised and conditioned to think of debt as a personal responsibility. Remember the definitions in the introduction? Paying off debt felt honorable, and defaulting on debt felt vaguely shameful. I remember watching a film about Mark Twain, made in the '40s I think, that dramatized the famous humorist going deeply into debt during his lifetime, being presented with the counseling of bankruptcy, and instead going on a year-long tour of speaking engagements, which he detested, to earn enough money to pay what he owed in full. It was inspiring and drove home the concept of responsibility for one's own finances. I wanted to be that guy. I had taken out the loans, and I wanted to pay them back.

In addition to my sense of failure, I was self-judgmental. How could I be forty years old and looking at bankruptcy? How did it come to that? I had always been responsible with money, never living beyond my means. I had never carried more than $10,000 in credit-card debt and usually paid off my balances in full each month. I had always earned a decent living, was responsible with my spending, and proud of my 800 FICO score. How could I have come to this?

My turmoil was not only psychological, but physical and emotional, too. It was an effort to eat well and exercise regularly, though I knew if I let those things go, my health would quickly deteriorate. I could feel a despondency setting in that I didn't want to call depression. I wouldn't sleep well at night and would then spend too much time in bed in the morning out of some intangible sense of inability to do anything to help my situation. I was overwhelmed.

Moreover, I was in great doubt as a person and as a man. I had been dating a wonderful woman for about eight months and found myself having extreme difficulty maintaining the relationship. I began to feel like I had nothing to offer her while I was so upside down in my finances. I fretted over going out to dinner or even going to the movies at $14 a ticket in Los Angeles. She was in love with me, and I drove her away because I felt, somehow, incapable of returning her love while my debt weighed so heavily upon me every day.

My debt situation had turned into the "story" of my life. You know the "story," the defining elements of your life that you rattle off spontaneously each time someone asks, "How's it going?"

Whenever I would meet a friend for a drink or lunch, it was the same thing. "I'm in debt, a lot of debt. The movie isn't selling. I've only got enough money for a few more months. Then, I don't know what I'm going to do. I'm afraid I'm going to lose my house. I'm not dating. I don't feel that I have anything to offer a woman. How did my life get here?"

It really was nauseating. It's difficult to recall it without feeling sick. I feel sorry for my friends and family who had to listen to it so many times. And most of the time, the person opposite the lunch table would offer to pick up the bill, and I would feel more pathetic because saving ten bucks wasn't going to change my situation, and yet, I certainly seemed to be pleading for that kind of assistance. So, wishing to avoid that pathetic feeling, I would try not to tell the story, which left a different kind of awkwardness. "How's it going?" "Fine."

My friends knew I wasn't fine. I didn't look fine. My face and body didn't say I was fine. And yet, fine I was, by default. A tough choice, between pathetic and falsely fine.

So, with great help and support from my family and friends, I took a serious look at the pity-pot I was sitting on. What did it get me, this depression, this sense of failure? Nothing tangible. Oh, a few ten-buck lunches, sure, and a lot of sympathy; but no respect, no lessons, no dates, no eagerness among my friends to spend time with me. Certainly no business.

It was time to get in touch with what I did have. I had a finished cut of a movie that I'd spent two years working on. And I had a choice. Throughout my career, whenever I was on a movie set and things were "going wrong," such as too much rain, lights blowing out, crew lost in traffic, running out of film, I would say loudly, "These are the problems I choose." It was my way of acknowledging that every business comes with problems. It is impossible to go through life without things "going wrong." I would get in touch with just how much I enjoyed filmmaking and acknowledge that, problems or not, I was happy to be where I was, happy to be experiencing the problems I had rather than the problems that an accountant or say, a collection agent might have. I had lost sight of that philosophy, and my "story" had become about debt. But really, I was just in another (heretofore unexperienced) problem of filmmaking, being in debt after the production.

There's an analogy I've always liked that highlights the choice we have when facing a pitfall in life. Skiers and snowboarders will appreciate it. When you're going down that big hill, wind blowing through your hair, an exhilarating chill on your cheeks, and you fall, a big, tumbling, embarrassing fall that gets the people on the lift looking down at you and laughing, you have a choice. You can get angry, kick off your skis, stomp into the lodge for a Jack Daniel's and hot chocolate, and call it a bitter day, or you can laugh, grin, smile at the great run you had, strap your skis back on, and keep going for the rest of the slope.

I was down, no doubt, and I didn't know how I was going to get back up again. I wasn't going to call it a day in the lodge, and I had a choice about how I was going to live my life during this crisis.

I call it a context change. I changed my context from depressed and emotional to "This is the mountain I'm on, and I'm going to ski it as best I can." It had been my choice to finish the film, my choice to put my own money into it. I had opportunities to learn and grow, and I would embrace them instead of denying them. I chose to change my story from "Woe is me. How did I end up here?" to "Let's live this journey for all it's worth."

Debt would not be reason enough to stop me from enjoying my life.

Let's start doing the work. At the end of each chapter, I'm going to offer a "Worksheet" that will not only highlight important concepts, but also ask you important questions about your situation. The questions may seem simple, but answering them for yourself, as you will see, can lead to a much better chance of success when it comes to talking to collection agents and settling debt.

WORKSHEET MY "STORY"

➤ What is your "story?"

➤ How is it serving you?

➤ What negative context are you carrying?

➤ How can you change it to make it positive?

Chapter 2

BANKRUPTCY?

THOUGH I HAD A NEW context, my situation had not tangibly changed. Faster and faster I felt myself slipping toward that unimaginable quicksand known as "bankruptcy." Just the term "bankruptcy" brought back the feelings of failure, somehow tied to painful memories of losing at Monopoly when I was a child. As an adult, I realized that I didn't even really know what bankruptcy meant.

On the advice of my family, I visited a bankruptcy attorney who was recommended through my accountant. Here is how I understood his explanation: In 2005, President Bush signed the Bankruptcy Abuse Prevention and Consumer Protection Act of 2005,[1] which made it substantially more difficult for an individual to file Chapter 7 bankruptcy (in which debts could be expunged) and provided several tests designed to steer more individuals toward Chapter 11 and Chapter 13 bankruptcy, which require structured repayment of debts.[2] Although any bankruptcy filing would stop

---

[1] For more information, try *http://www.nacm.org/resource/Bankruptcy-Act_apr15-05.html* or *www.cch.com/bankruptcy/bankruptcy_04-21.pdf*, which are simply Web links I found doing a Google search.

[2] For more information on the different "chapters" of bankruptcy, I recommend you turn to many sources (books, websites, legal counsel, accountants, etc.) that can provide more detailed and accurate information than I on the subject.

all collection attempts, phone calls, and legal proceedings, as I understood my attorney, even a Chapter 7 filing would no longer simply wipe away all credit-card debt. Instead, when one files bankruptcy, he or she goes into a kind of financial receivership. The court appoints a single person (whom my attorney calls a "Super Creditor") to take control of all of the person's finances. The "Super Creditor" has the ability to liquidate assets (bank accounts, stocks and bonds, other investments, even homes and automobiles under certain conditions) and decide how and to whom to dispense the cash to pay off debts. A person filing bankruptcy is allowed to keep up to approximately $22,000.[3]

My understanding is that this new scope of the bankruptcy law was intended to protect lenders from situations in which people may have tens or hundreds of thousands of dollars or more in assets, as well as tens or hundreds of thousands of dollars or more of debt, and rather than pay off their debt with their assets, they would file bankruptcy, wipe out their debt, and be allowed to keep their assets.

The new law clearly favors the lenders when a debtor has large assets. If a debtor has little in assets (such as is my case, and perhaps yours), a bankruptcy turned over to a "Super Creditor" may result in the creditors receiving little toward the outstanding debt.

With about $50,000 in cash and a car worth maybe $18,000, a house with no equity, and $212,000 of debt, no one was going to get much if I went into bankruptcy. Still, I asked my attorney if there was an option for me that did not involve filing bankruptcy.

His answer was something I never expected. Something

---

[3] I live in California. It is possible that these details differ in other states.

I'd never before heard. Moreover, his answer changed my life.

My attorney told me that I could negotiate with the banks that issued my credit cards to settle my debt for less than I owed. Strangely, this seems like common knowledge today after the proliferation of radio and television commercials for debt settlement that have arisen since the autumn 2008 TARP Bailout. In 2007, these practices were not yet widely advertised. Perhaps you have heard of this concept before. Perhaps you or someone you know has done it. It was entirely new to me. Negotiating debt? What did that mean?

In the introduction, I listed the dictionary definitions of debt. There were two. A money debt and an obligation to another person.

There is a third definition, I have discovered, that is not printed in Webster's. To the financial world, debt is an entirely different thing. Debt is a commodity. An asset to be bought and sold like stock. In fact, as I learned, the entire United States financial system is based on debt. Not cash, debt.

When a person buys a house, or more properly, secures a loan to buy a house, that loan, say for $1 million, is entered onto the bank's account sheet as an asset. The buyer's debt is an asset for the bank. If you've bought a home, you may have seen your mortgage holder change during the term of the loan. That change of note holder represents one bank selling your debt, their asset, to another bank.

Many collection agencies are in the business of buying debt. They buy it in bulk at pennies on the dollar, then do the work of collecting whatever they can on the outstanding notes. If they can settle with you at 80, 70, 60 percent of what you originally owed, they see a profit if they bought the debt for 5 to 10 percent of its "value."

Thus, as a record number of credit-card balances fall thirty, sixty, ninety days past due, increasing numbers of homeowners go into foreclosure, and more people and businesses file bankruptcy, banks are motivated to settle a debt for 60, 40, even 20 percent of what is owed before they sell it for 5 to 10 percent to a collection agency, or potentially lose it all if the customer files bankruptcy. I would speculate that in the current economy, many banks, especially those on the brink of insolvency themselves, are more motivated than ever to settle your debt.

I have a feeling that many readers may be thinking, or even saying aloud, "Okay, the banks want to settle my debt, but do I?" I understand the dilemma. Debt is an emotional issue, and it stands to reason that the concept of settling debt would stir up emotion, as well. It did for me. At first, I didn't take to the idea of settling my debt for less than I owed. I had never intentionally missed a monthly credit-card payment in more than twenty years of being a cardholder. Never a bank card, gasoline card, or department-store card. I still wanted to be Mark Twain. I wanted to sell the film and pay everyone back. I wanted to feel good about myself and honor my debts. I wanted . . . I wanted . . . I wanted. I wanted to be six feet tall. I only made it to 5 feet 5 inches.

Okay. I took a deep breath and got realistic about my situation. I could stand on my sense of integrity and keep shelling out $3,600 a month in minimum payments while I hoped that the Hollywood union labor disputes ended and the economy and housing market turned around before I spent the last of my savings. Or I could take action in a direction that just might get me through this situation without filing bankruptcy or becoming homeless.

"If I am going to negotiate with my creditors," I asked my attorney hesitantly, "how is it done?"

His answer surprised me. He said that banks and credit-card issuers are more likely to negotiate with someone who is behind in their monthly payments than with someone who is current. Apparently, banks are more apt to believe that an individual is close to filing bankruptcy and that they may not get anything at all if that individual is not making his or her monthly payments. I gathered — and found to be true over time — that when it comes to nego-tiating, banks are testing your resolve. I imagine (I choose that word intentionally, this is true imagination as I have never asked a bank to confirm this) that they figure if one is willing to go through all it takes to get to the point of a settlement, then that person must truly be in financial dif-ficulty, for no one would want to go through the process if he or she had the ability to continue making payments and settle their debt.

I asked my attorney to what extent he felt my creditors might be willing to settle, i.e., at what percentage of what I owed. He said that it varied depending on the bank and how they perceived a particular debtor's situation. He thought that 50 percent was not uncommon, perhaps even less. I sighed. Even 50 percent of what I owed was still more than $100,000. Even if all they took was 25 percent, that would leave me with not a dime to live on.

There was another consideration. My credit score. "What will that do to my credit?"

I learned that most banks will wait through about three to six months of delinquent payments before charging off the account (sending it to collections). Meaning, at first, that not making my monthly payments wouldn't do anything to my credit, at least for a little while.

And for me, there was an additional benefit. Not spending $3,600 a month on credit-card payments would increase the amount of time I could live on my savings from six months to nearly ten. That was almost a year to sell the film and pay off the debt, perhaps even before I took a credit hit.

Not knowing if I would really be able to negotiate settlements with my creditors, I followed my attorney's advice and stopped making payments.

Then the phone calls started.

WORKSHEET: **BANKRUPTCY?"**

➤ Do your own research. Being informed on all your options, including bankruptcy, will help you determine whether debt settlement is the right approach for your situation.

➤ Seek professional counseling from your own tax accountant and bankruptcy attorney.

➤ Make a spreadsheet of your finances. Include your monthly income, total monthly expenses, and the portion of expenses that is credit-card payments to determine how much money you may be able to put toward settlements.

➤ Ask yourself if you can live with a credit-score hit. Are you planning to buy a new home, new car, take out a second mortgage to send a child to college? If you're not planning to use your credit score soon, can you live with it lowering for a while to get you through the immediate crisis?

Chapter 3

COLLECTIONS

THE DEBT I CARRIED WAS spread over seven different credit cards and business lines of credit at six banks. I am not going to identify the banks individually. However, I will say that all of my creditors were major U.S. banks or credit-card issuers such as American Express, Bank of America, Capital One, Chase, Citibank, Comerica, Countrywide, Discover, National City Bank, USAA, Wachovia, Washington Mutual, or Wells Fargo.

I have applied non-descriptive, completely fictitious names to the banks that follow for the purpose of describing my dealings with individual institutions.

The banks and amounts I owed to each were:

Yellow Bank	$76,000
Red Bank	$24,000
Blue Bank	$21,000
Green Bank	$17,500
White Bank	$12,500
Brown Bank 1	$22,000
Brown Bank 2	$39,000
Total:	**$212,000**

I stopped making payments on five of the seven cards in January 2008. Green Bank and White Bank, the two with the lowest balances and therefore lowest monthly payments, I kept current out of the sheer need in our society to have plastic available, if only for emergencies and not to carry lots of cash around.

There was a deceivingly quiet period that followed immediately after I stopped making my payments on the other five cards. It had to do with timing. As an example, let's say I didn't make a January 1 payment on a card. As a good customer with a long history of paying my credit cards on time, I did not receive a collections call for one late payment. On my next bill, the previous month's payment was listed as past due and added to the current month's payment along with a late fee (thirty-nine bucks, ouch!). The banks gave me about two more weeks, until my billing approached the next cycle, before giving me a "courtesy" call.

I suppose I had expected abrasive people demanding payment with threats, but everyone on these early calls was nice. A typical call would go something like this:

The phone rings. I answer. "Hello."[4]

Nothing on the other line. Anyone who has ever answered a computer-generated call knows this pause.

I would say again, "Hello."

"Good morning, sir. How are you today?"

I always had trouble answering this one. They knew I was behind in a payment, so saying I was doing great wasn't exactly true, but no one wants to launch into a sob story. So, "fine" usually sufficed. "How are you?" is usually perfunctory anyway.

---

[4] I'll use quotes to signify the person on the other end of the phone speaking, though I am paraphrasing the content and not suggesting that these are actual quotes of the exact words said.

"This is "Kevin" calling from card services—"[5]

They never offered the name of the bank they were calling from. I'm guessing it is training they receive because none of my creditors would ever identify which bank they were calling from without my asking. Upon my asking, they were always forthright.

"Card services from which bank?"

"This is Yellow Bank calling about your Visa ending in XXXX."

"Okay, thank you."

"You're aware that your last payment of $800 was due on the first of February?"

They all asked if I was aware of my past-due payment. All of them. I feel confident in saying that I am not just relaying an anecdote here, but actually describing the process that you might experience in the same situation. This pattern of call was consistent for all the banks.

"Yes, Kevin, I am aware."

"Okay, well, we're calling to set up that payment today."

Also part of the technique. They would never ask me if I could make the payment, it seems to me, because it makes it easy to say, "No, I can't." They would simply state that they were calling to set up the payment, as if there were no other option. I found it very well-thought out.

From the first call, I had to figure out how I was going to handle them. I did not want to be confrontational. I did not want to express any anger. In fact, I was clear that I had nothing to be angry about. I knew that they had the right to call me and ask for my payment, which was in fact past due.

---

[5] I have changed his name, as with all the names I use herein, except mine.

Many books on debt advise the contrary—to deny your debt when called. I chose to admit to the debt as I found it healthier for me, mentally, emotionally, and physically, to "own" that I had made these charges and admit that I was in an unexpected situation that required me to stop making payments for the moment. Personally, I found that the calls went more smoothly when I was honest and forthright than I feel they would have gone had I been evasive.

"I appreciate your call, Kevin, and I'd love to make that payment today, but I am unable to."

Next step, consistently, every call, every bank:

"I see that you have a great credit score and a solid payment history. Can I ask what it is that has caused you to fall behind in your payments?"

"Sure, Kevin, thanks for asking. I went into a business venture with a partner, and it went substantially over budget. My partner, who provided the financing, then took unexpectedly ill and died, leaving me with debt that I didn't anticipate. In addition, I work in the entertainment industry, and we're in the middle of a long Writers Guild strike. So I have had difficulty finding work in the past few months. I'm living off savings and have had to make some very hard choices about where to put my quickly dwindling resources. I'm trying to sell my house, though I'm not getting any interest in this market. Believe me, Kevin, I like my 800 credit score, and if I could, I would certainly make this payment instead of having this phone call."

At this point, the agent would almost always say, "I'm very sorry to hear about your troubles. I hope things get better for you. You next payment of $XXX is due on March 1. You will continue to receive these calls until your account is brought current. Have a good day."

Not a bad phone call, all things considered. Except that I had five cards I wasn't making payments on. I would receive three to five calls every two to three days. Often, because I had two cards with Brown bank, I would have the conversation with someone about one of the cards, hang up, and seconds later get a call from the same bank to have the same conversation about the second card.

It didn't take long to make a list of area codes and phone numbers for the various banks. None were "unknown" or blocked numbers. I never avoided talking to them entirely. However, when I was busy, working on selling the film, writing, or just trying to look toward the future, I would take a break and not answer now and then.

Of note, they never, ever left messages. Of course not. The initial call was generated by a computer. Remember the pause? Only after a second "hello" would an actual person come on the line. When no one answered, the computer just rolled to the next number.

These calls continued for about four months with nothing changing. I didn't have enough money to engage in settlement negotiations, so that process had not yet begun. Week after week, I would receive the phone calls, always the same pattern as described above, always with a different person who may or may not have had all my information on a computer screen in front of him or her. It didn't matter. The phone calls were regular and always the same.

In April of 2008, something different happened.

I received my monthly statement from Yellow Bank and was shocked to see that I had $2,500 less than I thought in my business savings account. It didn't take long to figure out that Yellow Bank had unilaterally withdrawn the last three, past-due payments on my business line of credit directly from my savings account. After suffering heart palpitations and indignation (a somewhat false indignation, I'll admit, but nonetheless, it felt real at the time), I found my original application and confirmed that it included a clause allowing them to automatically withdraw past due payments from my account.

Knowing that I was not going to make the next payment, and now knowing that when I didn't Yellow Bank would make its own withdrawal again, I drove to the nearest branch of a major bank that was not one of my creditors and opened an account. I then drove across the street to Yellow Bank and withdrew my savings in cash, then drove back across the street to deposit the cash in my new account. Lesson learned.

In May 2008, I received a gift. My business partner, Gabe, had left his estate, along with his interest in the film, to his nephew, who called me out of the blue to say that he would be able to put an additional $45,000 into the production company to help settle some of the credit-card debt. To this day and forever, I will not be able to express my gratitude to him for this gesture. He had no obligation to do this. His motivation was simple goodness. He wanted to thank me for the enjoyment that I had provided his uncle toward the end of his life, and I am deeply thankful to him for that gesture.

Even though the $45,000 would tackle only a portion of my debt, I felt that I could begin to negotiate settlements without depleting my savings, which I would still use to pay my mortgage, my utilities, and for food.

I returned to my bankruptcy attorney to say that we could start the process of negotiations. I chose to have him focus on my two largest creditors, Yellow Bank with a $76,000 balance, and Brown Bank, which had two cards, one for $22,000 and one for $39,000. If we could settle the entire

$137,000 for 33%, it would be a good use of the $45,000 and would reduce my overall debt to only $75,000, from $212,000.

The first step with the attorney was to fill out a form that he would send to the two banks showing them that he had the authority to discuss my accounts on my behalf. What was surprising to me was that neither bank wanted to talk to him. They continued calling me. I would tell them that I had engaged a bankruptcy attorney to discuss a settlement with them. Still neither bank would call him. When he called them, they did not respond. I gathered that banks generally are more successful negotiating higher settlements when they speak directly to the borrower, who, like me, is often more emotional about the situation and more likely to agree to a higher percentage. An attorney can be more removed and ideally, a better negotiator for the client.

After a couple of weeks, this tactic of not talking to my attorney actually worked. I found myself getting anxious to see some progress in reducing my debt and so when they called, I began to say that I was open to a settlement payment.

As soon as I said "settlement," the conversation with the banks changed. The calls started off with the same, cordial, "How are you today?" "We're calling to set up a payment." "How did you get behind in your payments?" Then, instead of giving my story and telling them I was unable to make a payment, I would say that I wanted to reach a settlement, and the person on the other side of the call seemed to get excited. I wonder if they work on commission. I don't know. But they seemed to be more engaged in the conversation, less rote, a little more scattered, a little more human. They would immediately ask me how much I was offering in settlement.

Hoping to settle at 33 percent, I started by offering 20 percent. Both Yellow and Brown Bank said that they never take settlements of 20 percent. Brown said they "begin" settlement negotiations at 85 percent. Yellow said they "begin" at 92 percent. That tickled my funny bone. I said, "92 percent of $76,000 is about $70,000. If I had $70,000 to send you, do you think I'd be four months behind in my payments?" In any case, I didn't have 92 or 85 percent, and the conversations would end with them telling me I would continue to receive the phone calls and that they hoped things would get better for me.

I liked that they both used the word "begin." I was already seeing many patterns in the scripting and language that the various callers from the different banks used. I hung up from those first couple of calls anticipating rapid progress. Silly me.

As my attorney had warned, the process took several months. Each bank would call two to three times a week. They would, as usual, begin by telling me they were calling to set up a payment on the past due amount. I would tell them that when I last spoke to them I had offered a settlement of 20 percent. They would repeat that they never go that low and tell me the calls would keep coming.

After about a month of stalemate for both cards, I seemed to enter the next "round." When I said I could offer 20 percent, Brown came back with an offer of 55. I was surprised at how easily they'd dropped from 85 percent to 55. I'd said no to 85 percent, didn't budge for a month, and now they were calling back at 55 percent. Something clicked for me. They had a pattern, a script, and as the script moved to the next lower stage, their level of cordiality dropped also. At the higher percentage, they were nice, ending the calls with

"Have a nice day" and "We hope things get better for you." As if being nice might induce me to accept their high offer.

I'm guessing that being less nice as the percentage drops is the next step in their training procedure. These callers were not surprised by my offer to settle, but prepared for it. They would tell me that if I didn't settle now, the account could go into "charge off," when the bank turns the debt over to a collection agency. They said that they had not yet reported my delinquency to the credit bureaus, but if the account went into charge off, it would hurt my credit score and impede my ability to buy a house or a car. They insisted that I had signed an agreement to make regular payments on my loan and then questioned my honor and my integrity, insinuating that I was a bad person for not paying off my debt. This was the first time that a caller had turned the conversation personal. I'll admit it was effective. I struggled with the contradiction between living up to my word and doing what had to be done not to become broke and homeless.[6]

---

[6] See the later chapter, *The Debt Double Standard*, for more thoughts on this subject.

WORKSHEET: "COLLECTIONS"

➤ Using the financial chart you did in the last worksheet and how much money you are able to put toward settlement payments, calculate the percentage and dollar amount you will take on each account so you know what you are aiming for in your negotiations. Don't just "go fishing" for a good offer.

➤ If you have deposit accounts at the same bank you owe money to, are not making payments to, and are attempting to settle with, consider opening an account at a new bank and moving your savings away from the bank you are negotiating with.

➤ Be prepared for the tone of the calls to escalate as the percentage offers drop and for them to tell you all the bad things that will happen to you if you don't make payments or accept their settlement offers. Their goal is to rile you.

➤ Be pleasant and forthright during the collection calls. Don't let them get you emotionally off guard.

➤ Save the numbers they call from so you can recognize them when they call and be prepared when you answer.

Chapter 4

FALSE START

OVER THE NEXT FEW MONTHS, I received regular calls regarding the five credit-card accounts on which I had stopped making my monthly payments. So that I could focus my attention on Yellow and Brown banks, when I received calls from Red and Blue banks, I would once again say that I was not in a position to make a payment, that I was trying to sell my house, and I was looking forward to resuming payments when it was possible.

To Yellow Bank (with a $76,000 balance) and Brown Bank (with two cards, one for $22,000 and the other for $39,000), I continued offering 20 percent as a settlement. As I said, my goal was 33 percent, and I felt that if I jumped to 25 or 30 percent too quickly, they wouldn't come below 40 to 45 percent. I had no evidence for that, it was just a feeling. Brown Bank called often, sometimes back to back on the two different accounts, as I've said. We were stuck at 55 percent on their end, and the calls were making no further progress.

During this period, I had a very unusual call from Yellow Bank. It was far less friendly than most of the calls I'd received from all my creditors. The man on the phone said, "You need to take care of this," and "Do whatever you have to do to take care of this debt."

I told him my story; the business debt that I had taken on and why, the death of my partner, the Writers Guild strike, Screen Actors Guild dispute, the general economy, mortgage and credit crises, and that I'd been trying to sell my house to no avail.

In response, he said, "Take a short sale on your house."

I was a little irritated that he would tell me how to handle the sale of my house, but I got past that with the understanding that he was just doing his job for his company, pursuing their best interests. What riled me was that the suggestion made no sense.

A short sale is when one sells a house for less than it is worth and asks the mortgage holder to write off the difference so that you can walk away from the house without owing anything.

"How will a short sale help this situation?" I asked him.

"I'm not here to tell you how it will help, only to say that you need to do it."

"I don't get it," I said. And I really didn't get it. I had been trying to sell my house for ten months hoping for as much as $100,000 in profit so that I could use that money to pay off or settle more of my debt. But a short sale would realize no profit for me, and therefore no new ability to pay on the debt. So I didn't see how the suggestion was relevant. It seemed to me like he had a script in front of him that had several suggestions of statements to throw at people, only he didn't know it very well, or didn't understand it very well, and wasn't willing (or had been told not to) admit the mistake and move past it. He just switched back to "You need to take care of this." The call ended with my saying that I'd retained a bankruptcy attorney and he should call him.

For the first time, a bank actually called my attorney. The

Yellow Bank agent he spoke with said that to entertain a settlement, they needed me to fill out a questionnaire with all of my financial details. It requested my total income, savings, assets, stocks, cars, house, mortgage, credit-card balances and monthly payments, the whole thing.

I was uncomfortable with their request. There was something awkward about approaching a negotiation by telling the other party everything I had, kind of like showing my cards before the final bet at the poker table. My overall goal was to settle with both Yellow and Brown Banks with the $45,000 that my late business partner's heir had contributed, while retaining the $35,000 left in my own savings (down from $50,000 after several months of living expenses) to continue living on while I sought to sell the film and look for work. However, considering the perspective of Yellow Bank, showing them that I had $80,000 in cash might (I felt would) make them feel that I had enough money to pay off their entire loan in full ($76,000) and not induce them to settle.

All this "strategizing" ended when my attorney pointed out that if I did not provide my financial information to the bank, they would refuse to negotiate, which is the same outcome as if I did provide the information and upon looking at the numbers, they refused to negotiate. At least if I filled out their form, there was the chance they would negotiate. So, despite my feeling like I was showing my hand too early, there was nothing to lose in filling out the form as an inducement to settle.

We sent in the form and never heard back. No response, either positive or negative. They didn't return further calls from my attorney. They stopped calling me. I have no explanation for this.

Brown Bank had not stopped calling. One of the great frustrations I had with Brown Bank was that I had two separate cards with them, the $22,000 balance on a personal card and the $39,000 on a business card. I would have loved to have been able to speak with one person about both accounts and settle them together, but there seemed to be no way to get anyone on the bank's side to do that. Moreover, it was impossible even to get the same person on the phone twice at Brown Bank. Their employees did not have extensions. Whenever I called them, I had to take whomever came on the phone and explain my entire situation anew. They seemed to have notes on their computer for my account, but it was still a tedious process of bringing each new person up to speed rather than having one representative assigned to both accounts.

At one point, Brown Bank's offer on the personal card came down from 55 percent to slightly less than 50 percent, $10,000 to settle the $22,000 balance. I was offering $4,000, and my goal was to settle at $7,000. The difference between their offer and my target was only $3,000, and I was tempted to accept what they had placed on the table. I dearly wished to begin seeing this process work, to settle with even one card and know that I was making progress toward bringing down my overwhelming debt. I held firm, though, believing that if I took their approximately 50-percent offer on this card, that might give them a stronger leverage in demanding 50 percent on their other card. That would mean roughly $31,000 on the overall $62,000 with Brown Bank, instead of my goal of $21,000, which would leave me only $15,000 to settle the $76,000 with Yellow Bank, and that seemed terribly unlikely. I found strength in my commitment to settle not just a portion of my debt, but to settle all of my debt. By holding fast to that goal, it was easier for me to refuse the 50 percent. I had already seen how they came down from 85 percent, so I felt confident there was another rung for them to take.

Brown Bank took out a new tool from the box at this point. On the next call, when I again offered 20 percent, I was told that the account was in "pre-legal," meaning it would soon go to their legal department to pursue a lawsuit against me. "If" that happened ("if," not "when," I noted, to give me the opportunity to avoid it), they assured me that I would "no longer be able to negotiate." I would "be responsible for the entire balance in full immediately, plus legal fees," and I would "have a judgment against me" that would allow them "to garnish my wages," "attach my bank accounts," and "put a lien on my house." All of these intimidations did rattle me, I'll admit, but for the time being, Brown Bank was still negotiating, offering the same $10,000 on the personal card, and I felt I had some time to bring that down before it progressed to a lawsuit.

In mid-June, after three months of negotiating with no results, I saw my first glimmer of hope. This time, Brown Bank offered 35 percent on the business card with the $39,000 balance, a settlement of $13,656. That seemed pretty good. It was very close to my 33-percent target. Before taking it immediately, I choose to see what kind of leeway there was still. I said that I really appreciated their working with me in that way. I had been offering 20 percent, so in recognition of their being open, I would bring my offer up to 25 percent. It seemed reasonable to me that if they would take $13,656, they would take $10,000. Again, though it seemed like a small difference between their offer and mine, saving $4,000 here would allow me to offer a couple thousand more on the

36 THE DO IT YOURSELF BAILOUT

personal card and possibly settle both with Brown Bank at or close to my target of $21,000.

A couple of weeks later, I received a letter in the mail denying the offer. (See Document 1)

July 06, 2008

Mr Kenneth Golde

**Important information is
provided below regarding
your account.**

RE: Your account ending in

Dear Mr Kenneth Golde:

We have reviewed your request to settle your credit card account. We appreciate the effort that you are making to pay down your outstanding balance. Unfortunately, we have determined that your account does not qualify for a settlement at this time.

We may have another payment option that is right for you. Or, if you are interested in learning more about non-profit credit counseling agencies, please call us toll-free today at 1-877-

Sincerely,

Customer Support Division

Document 1: Initial offer refusal from "Brown" Bank

I was not deterred. It was clear to me that this was simply a negotiating tactic, that the bank still felt I was not in dire-enough financial straits to warrant their taking less than their 35-percent offer as a settlement on my business account. I called back to see if we could meet in-between their offer of $13,656 and mine of $10,000. Now remember, it was impossible to ever get the same person on the phone at this bank. They had no extensions, no last names. Whenever I called, I would enter my account number and social security number and get transferred to a department. So I did that, entering the account number for the card with the $39,000 balance. I got someone on the phone, repeated the history of the two offers, and said I would meet in the middle at $12,000. She was happy to accept my offer of $12,000, and I was ecstatic. I felt, finally, that this process had merit, was real, and I saw a true, proven path to getting through this crisis that had left me feeling so crippled for a full year now.

My attorney had prepared me for this moment, stating emphatically that I should send no money in settlement of an account without first receiving a settlement agreement, in writing, stating the terms. I asked for such a letter to be faxed to me. The agent said she could do that. She just wanted to take a recording of my agreement so that it was finalized on their end. She started her tape recorder. I stated my name and address and that I was prepared to send them $12,000 as settlement in full on account XXXX with a balance of $39,000 upon receiving a letter confirming—

She stopped me to say that this was for the other card, the card with the $22,000 balance. "No!" I exclaimed. "I entered the account number for the business card when I called back. I'm offering the $12,000 settlement on the $39,000 balance, not the $22,000 balance. You already offered me $10,000 on that card, why would I offer you $12,000 now?"

She was nice about it. She agreed that there was quite a lot of confusion owing to the fact that I had two cards with the same bank, in different departments that couldn't communicate with each other. She apologized for the confusion, but the deal would not go through.

Ugh!

Deep breath.

I felt like a baseball fan hearing the crack of the bat, watching the ball sail high into the sky where it gets lost against the lights, then reappear heading toward the fence. A Home

Run! Only to be snagged by the center fielder and brought back into play. An out. My shoulders sagged. Would I ever get through this? She reiterated that the personal account with the $22,000 balance was in "pre-legal" and this might be my last opportunity to settle before being sued. I could still accept their $10,000 offer.

Here again is why they make it so difficult for my attorney to talk to them. With instructions to settle at $7,000, he would have no problem refusing. I, on the other hand, found my new context of living my life fully with the debt rather than letting the debt define my life to be challenged, to wane. I fell back into my old depression a bit and had the fear renewed within me. It was all I could do to get off the phone without saying, "Yes."

A few days later, while still brooding in medium despondence, I got a call from Brown on the $39,000 card (funny how I couldn't reach them, but they could reach me), offering the 35 percent again — $13,656. The last time I'd spoken to them and offered $10,000, I was feeling strong and enjoying negotiating for negotiations sake. Now I was weaker. After the confusion and disappointment when I'd tried to offer $12,000, this time I took the $13,656 proposal. I wanted some progress, some movement, some success.

If I'd thought the guys on the phone got excited in the early days when I said I was willing to settle, this guy's tone when I said I'd go for the $13,656 was what I can only describe as giddy. They must be on commission. He was aflutter. "Um, okay, lemme see, I think I have to, can I put you on hold, please?"

"Of course." So hold I did for several minutes. He finally returned to the phone a bit calmer, more centered, breathing, and said he'd talked to his supervisor (called a "gatekeeper"), the offer was approved, and he could set up a telephone transfer of the payment right then.

Not so fast, bucko. I told the giddy guy on the phone that I had the money and was prepared to make the transfer upon receipt of a letter stating that we had reached a settlement agreement, that the sum received was to be deemed payment in full on the account, and that no further collections or legal action would be taken.

He said I would receive that letter after I made the payment. For the first time in all of these calls, I found myself losing the calm, pleasantry that I had managed to maintain thus far. "Why would I send the payment before having an agreement? That's silly. Would you pay for a new car, or a house, and then have them give you the purchase agreement to read over? Of course not. Send me the letter, by email, fax, or U.S. post, and I'll send the payment within five business days."

He put me on hold again. I waited. When he came back, he said okay, the letter can be sent. It had to be sent from a different department, and I would receive it by fax in a couple of days.

A couple of days passed. No fax. I called back. This is the bank that has no extensions, where I could never speak to the same person twice. The bank that, the last time I called about this account, I got sent to the other account. Guess what? Same thing. When someone came on the line, I said I wanted to confirm that I was talking about the business account with the $39,000 balance. She said no, the other one. "Can you please transfer me to someone on that account?" I asked.

"No."

"Really? So how do I talk to anyone about that account

if I can't get to it by entering that account number and you can't transfer me?"

She didn't know.

I was getting frustrated. A few days later, they called me on the business account, yet another new person whom I had to take through the whole history to the point where the deal was accepted and I was waiting for a confirmation letter. He said that according to the notes in my account, the letter had been sent. I said I'd never received it. He said he would put another note to send a letter, and I would get it in a couple of days. Merry-go-round.

A week later, they called again. Same rigmarole. Only this time the man on the phone said that the offer I made had never actually been accepted by a "gatekeeper." However, right now, he could officially accept it. The only problem was that in three days the account was scheduled for charge off, meaning it would either go to collections or legal, and this deal would no longer be valid. He stressed that I had to get my payment in before the charge off. I said, "Great, I can get my payment in today by wire transfer if you can get me the letter I've been promised for the last two weeks." He explained that the reason the letter never went out was that the deal had never actually been accepted (without explaining why it hadn't been accepted since I'd been told it had been accepted), but that now the letter could go out.

So I waited. Two days. Three days. I called again on the day the account was supposed to go into charge off and got through to the other account, but not this one. The day passed. I wasn't sure whether the account had actually gone into charge off. I'd been told by many of my banks that my credit-card accounts were due to go into charge off, but I kept getting the same calls for weeks and began to believe that the mysterious world of "charge off" was just another way to frighten me into making a payment.

A few days later, on August 4, I received a letter saying that the settlement offer had been accepted! The letter was written on July 28 and noted that payment had to be received by July 30, four days ago. By my math, it was most likely not even mailed until after the due date had passed. Some settlement.

---

rec'd 8/4/08

July 28, 2008

Mr Kenneth Golde

Important information is provided below regarding your account.

RE: Your account ending in

Dear Mr Kenneth Golde:

We are pleased to confirm that we've agreed to settle your credit card account for 13656. Our settlement brings you these three advantages:

- You will pay 13656, a significant savings over the full balance that you owe us*.
- We will stop all efforts to collect.
- We will report your account to the national credit bureaus as "settled"*.

Here is your schedule of payments that you have agreed to:

First Installment:	Due Date:	07/30/2008	Payment Amount:	13656
Second Installment:	Due Date:		Payment Amount:	
Third Installment:	Due Date:		Payment Amount:	
Fourth Installment:	Due Date:		Payment Amount:	

Please call 1-866-   toll-free to make payment arrangements, or you can mail us your payment to the address below. For your convenience, your first payment due will be given a 10-day grace period from the due date listed above. We must receive your payment before your grace period expires, or before the date your account is scheduled to charge off, whichever comes first. If you have any questions about your settlement agreement or, want to find out your charge off date, please call us at 1-866-

Until your settlement amount is paid in full, your Annual Percentage Rate will be 14.99%. This will have no impact on your settlement amount or payment(s). If you don't make each payment by its due date listed above, or we receive an insufficient payment (NSF), our settlement agreement will terminate and your account will revert to the terms of your Cardmember Agreement. If you are removed from the settlement plan, we'll continue our collection efforts and any payments made to that point would be applied to your full balance.

Document 2: "Bogus" acceptance letter from Brown Bank

After the fiasco of first thinking I'd reached a settlement, only to discover I'd been transferred to the wrong department and then again believing I'd reached a settlement, only to have the letter sent to me after the payment due date, my enthusiasm for the process was deteriorating.

The next day, I received a call from my first professional collection agent from a collection company, "Management Services." This wasn't a bank representative calling anymore. My attorney had explained to me that the banks themselves are often much easier to deal with in settlement negotiations than the collection companies because the banks are looking to cut their losses; whereas, the collection companies are looking to make a profit. This man was far more forceful on the phone. He showed none of the jittery nervousness of the call-center guys who got thrown off balance by a settlement offer. This guy was a pro. The stakes had gone up.[7]

He launched into a diatribe about how I was reneging on my loan agreement, how I was being dishonest, asking how could I expect to succeed in the world if I didn't take my debt seriously? Why should his "client" be asked to take a loss on the money they loaned me? Would I want to write off a loss on money that someone owed to me?

I didn't take any of this nearly as personally as I'd thought I would. I held onto my context that banks were in business just like me, and they were pursuing their best interests in their business just like I was pursuing my best interests in mine. I did ask him for some clarity on the type of collection company he worked for. Did they buy my debt and now

---

[7] The Fair Debt Collection Practices Act (FDCPA) governs the way third-party debt collectors can do business. A quick web search revealed the following, helpful article: *http://www.legalhelpers.com/bankruptcy-articles/fair-debt-collection-article.html.*

hold the note, or were they working on behalf of the bank to collect the debt? He said that they did not buy my debt, that they did work for the bank, and that in two days time, he had to make a recommendation to the bank on how to proceed with my account. I asked him what type of recommendations he would make. Did he recommend a settlement, legal action, continued collections? He was vague and changed the subject back to berating me.

I then told him that I had reached a settlement agreement on this account with the bank just days ago, but they weren't able to get me the written agreement prior to the account going into charge off. He said that his guess was the gatekeeper only agreed to that deal because he knew he wouldn't have to honor it, seeing that it would charge off in a few days. I offered to honor the settlement agreement sent to me. He said that there was no way they would honor it. They would generously take my $13,656 payment against the total and put me on a payment plan for the full balance. I said I wasn't comfortable going onto a payment plan when I still had no expectation of regular income soon, was living off savings, and didn't see myself in the near future as any more able to make regular payments than I had been over the last eight months.

He told me that I had forty-eight hours to accept his offer or he would make the recommendation to his client that they take further action, without clarifying what "further action" meant.

Two days later, he called back. I reiterated that I would honor the agreement offered by Brown Bank before the charge off. He refused, and I assumed that meant he was going to make his recommendation to his client. But a week later, he called again. This time I was able to honestly say, "I don't know why you are calling. I thought you had to make your recommendation to the bank after the first forty-eight hours." He avoided the comment like a politician avoids a question in a debate, slickly sidestepping and bringing the conversation back to how right he was and how wrong I was.

He then rattled off the names of all the banks I owed money to, how much I owed to them, and what payments I had or had not been making. This surprised me. I found myself indignant that he had all of this personal information. But then I saw it as relieving. I had nothing to hide, didn't need to eschew questions about where my debts were or what payments I was making. I found it a relief that he knew so much about my finances. I remembered the form that Yellow Bank had asked me to fill out and now realized that they, too, probably had most of the information available to them, credit-card balances, mortgage balance, everything but my savings accounts.

The collection agent then said something that actually helped me. He noted that I had been making regular payments to two of my creditors (White and Green banks) and asked why his client should be asked to take a large loss on their account while these other banks were getting paid. It was a good question. I explained that I had kept the accounts with the lowest balances and lowest monthly payments current so that I would still have access to the benefits of a credit card while struggling through my circumstances. I said that I wasn't certain how long I could continue to keep those cards current and that I may wind up, in the end, seeking a settlement with them, as well, which was true.

What I took from his point was that he would have more incentive to settle with me if all of my accounts were going past due. I hadn't considered that. I remembered what my attorney said about an individual bank being more likely to settle with me if my account was past due, but I hadn't considered that they would factor the status of my other accounts into the equation also.

I chose not to stop making payments on those cards at that time, but had an insight that was even more powerful. I realized that something had shifted in me. I was strategizing. This was no longer a situation where I was begging or pleading with the bank to do me the favor of reducing my debt. These situations had themselves become business transactions of their own accord, and I was treating them like any other negotiation in business.

WORKSHEET: "FALSE START"

➤ Remember that collection agents are just doing their job. The truth is, if they are calling you, you *are* behind in your payments, so don't take frustrations out on them.

➤ Don't make yourself wrong. Don't make the collection agent wrong. Get out of the conversation of right and wrong. Treat it all like a business negotiation because that's what it is.

➤ Know what percentage you are comfortable settling at, but also calculate the actual dollar amount if their offer is a bit higher. If you are going for 33 percent and their offer is 35, but that 2 percent is only a small amount, weigh the actual dollar figure difference against your willingness to continue the process.

➤ ALWAYS get a written settlement agreement stating the account number, total due, settlement amount, and the words "full settlement," "paid in full," or the like, approved by your attorney, BEFORE sending any money.

Chapter 5

THE MONEY ANGEL

A FEW DAYS LATER, I received a chain mail from a friend. We had lunch recently and shared our mutual financial worries. She's a lovely woman, one of those "light up a room" women, not only beautiful and sexy, but warm, open, powerful, friendly, and engaging. She makes everyone feel special and important, and people love to be around her. I wish I could be more like her. She told me the sad story of how she and her husband had to sell their house, and she was worried about the future, especially with a just-turned two-year-old.

This was early August of 2008. Gasoline was at $4.75 a gallon in L.A., and I had just filled my first-ever $70 tank, in a sedan, not an SUV. People all over the country were feeling the crunch. Food prices seemed to have doubled in a couple of months. President Bush's White House was denying any financial trouble in the country while John McCain and Barack Obama were figuring out how to address the faltering economy without scaring people. I was struggling through $212,000 in debt while trying to finish and sell my film so that I could turn my attention to other work.

In the spirit of hope, my friend sent me a chain mail of a Money Angel. Here is what it looked like:

This is a money angel.
Pass it to 6 of your good friends or family and be rich
in 4 Days. Pass it to 12 of your good friends or family
and be rich in 2 Days. I am not joking. You will find
an unexpected windfall. If you delete it, you will beg.

Trust me!!!

I am as skeptical as anyone when it comes to chain mails.
I've seen them all, the starving families, missing children,
luck, money, quotes from the Dalai Lama, stories, anecdotes,
wishes, spells and magic that clog up inboxes worldwide.

There was something about this one that spoke to me. I
was going to pass it on, I knew I was. And I wasn't going to
pass it on like a skeptic, explaining that it probably wouldn't
work but I'll give it a try, ho hum, ho hum.

I was going to "own" it.

I sent it to nineteen of my closest friends and family mem-
bers with the note:

I'm choosing to believe!!
Love and prosperity to you.

The very next morning I settled my first and largest credit
card account.

I owed $76,000 to Yellow Bank. My last intended pay-
ment was in January, eight months earlier, though you'll
recall they took an automated payment from my account
at their branch in April. I had last spoken to them about
two months earlier when they offered to settle at 92 percent (remember the ridiculous call about telling me to take
a short sale on my house?). I hadn't heard from them since
my attorney sent in the form requesting all of my financial
information.

The morning after I received and forwarded the money angel, I answered a call from a guy named "Stan" at "Recovery Services" company in New York. Stan said he was calling on behalf of Yellow Bank. I explained to him that months earlier I had offered to reach a negotiated settlement on the account. He asked how much I was offering. I said 25 percent (about $19,000). In hindsight, the reason I said 25 percent and not 20 was emotional. I had been unsuccessful in numerous negotiations with Brown Bank and was anxious to settle, so quickly and without thinking I upped my offer in the "hopes" that it would bring success. Another win for them on the "call the customer not the attorney" approach. Stan said he didn't think "they" would go for 25 percent, but that he'd take the offer in and see what "they" would say. I assumed that "they" meant the bank, though I wasn't certain and didn't ask whether this company had bought my debt or was only representing the bank.

The next morning, Stan called me back saying that "they" would take $27,000, 35.5 percent of the $76,000 balance. Wow! That was a far cry from 92 percent. I was as surprised as I was when Brown so quickly came down from 85 to 55 percent. Stan further offered, since I had said that I had the $19,000, that they would take $20,000 now and $7,000 in a month. My target for this bank had always been 33 percent, $25,000. I countered with $24,000, admitting that while $3,000 wasn't a large difference, it made a big difference to me (and hoping they would come back at my target of $25,000). I added, as an incentive, that I could pay it all at once, not partial now and the balance in a month. He said he'd have to "take it into them again" and would call me back.

It didn't take long for him to call me back, less than half an hour. I wonder what went on in that half hour. Did he talk to a manager or supervisor? Did he just get on the phone with someone else and then call me back to make it look like there was a conversation on the other side? Had he already been given parameters within which he knew he could settle? What was his bottom line—$20,000? $15,000? He was so quick to come back at $27,000 when I offered $19,000 that I'm fairly certain there was more leeway in there for me. When he called back, saying he had "just talked to the president," (president of what? his company? the national bank that carried my debt? the PTA?), he countered my $24,000 at $25,000, right on my target.

His additional condition was that they had to receive the payment no later than the next day. This was new for me. My attorney had indicated it was normal to have ten to fifteen business days to make such a payment, but Stan wanted it immediately. He suggested that they could do a phone transfer from my bank account, I could go into my bank to do a wire transfer, or overnight a cashier's check to them.

The easiest option seemed to be the phone transfer, but I wasn't ready to do it yet. I wanted a written agreement. I'd already been through the hassle with Brown Bank which said we'd had an agreement then wouldn't send paperwork, then said we didn't have an agreement, then we did, then sent expired paperwork.

Stan agreed to send a letter immediately. And he did. It came through by fax moments later and had all the language that seemed necessary, my account number, the total amount of the debt, the settlement amount, and the words "paid in full." (Document 3)

July 21, 2008

Kenneth Golde

Creditor
Claim Number:
Client Reference #:
Current Balance: $76,399.36
Settlement Offer: $25,000.00
Due Date: 08/13/08

Dear Mr. Golde:

This letter is to confirm that we will accept the amount indicated above as full settlement and release of your account provided said payment is received on or before the due date stated above. Upon clearance of your payment we will consider this account settled in full, mark our records accordingly as well as our clients.

Should the above stated terms and conditions not be met, we shall consider this offer withdrawn with the balance in full being due and payable and proceed with appropriate action without further notice to you.

This is an attempt to collect a debt and any information obtained will be used for that purpose. This communication is from a debt collector. Make your payment payable to the client listed above. The above file number should be listed on all correspondence and payments remitted to this office to ensure the proper handling and crediting of your account.

IN WITNESS WHEREOF, the parties have executed this Agreement as of the date and year set forth below.

Kenneth Golde
By:

Date: 8-12-08

Sincerely,

Document 3: First settlement agreement with Yellow Bank

I called my attorney to read him the letter. He confirmed that the letter contained all the language he required. Then something occurred to me. I realized that I didn't know "Stan" or his firm, "Recovery Services." I asked my attorney if he thought it would be necessary to call Yellow Bank to confirm that this person was indeed working for them.

Call it a little bit of paranoia, but something told me to do more due diligence. My attorney said he didn't think that would be necessary. He'd never known of a situation like this ever being fraudulent. Stan had my account number, my phone number, contact info, and the exact amount of my balance due. He must have been provided with all of that information by the bank, my attorney reasoned. I accepted that reasoning.

I was prepared to do the phone transfer, but I knew that it would require my giving them the routing number and account number of my new bank account. Remember, this is the same bank that made the automatic withdrawal from my account. I had removed all my money, and I wasn't thrilled with the idea of them knowing where my new accounts were and the account numbers.

I quickly went online and transferred just the amount of the settlement from my checking account into my nearly empty savings account at the new bank so that the transfer would only reveal an account that would have a nearly zero balance after the withdrawal. More paranoia, I know.

I called Stan back and gave him the routing number and account number. He said that they could not do a $25,000 transfer, but had to do five, $5,000 transfers. I said that would be fine. Then he put me on hold for a while, finally returning to say that he wasn't able to do the transfer and instead asked me to send a cashier's check or make a wire transfer.

More firecrackers were going off in my belly. This was a collection agency that worked for a bank. How was it possible that they couldn't do a telephone transfer? That's the business they are in, collecting money.

Still, my emotions were taking over. I was on the verge of

settling $76,000 for $25,000, reducing my overall debt from $212,000 to $136,000, a massive chunk.

I went to my bank branch and set up the wire transfer. Wire transfers in California have to be made before 2 p.m. or they do not go out until the next day. I got to the bank at 1:45 p.m. and tapped my feet anxiously as we filled out the paperwork. The account to which I was sending the money was at a bank in New York and in the name of the collection company, "Recovery Services," not in the name of Yellow Bank. We made the transfer, and I called Stan to tell him it had gone through, asking that in the morning, he confirm its receipt and send me a letter stating that it had been received and that the account was now settled in full. He agreed to do it.

The next morning I was flying to Northern California to celebrate a friend's fortieth birthday in the wine country of Sonoma. When my plane landed in Oakland, I called Stan to confirm that he had received the wire transfer and would send me a full release letter. I got his voice mail and left a message. A couple of hours later, I got to Sonoma and called again. Again, straight to voice mail. When I arrived at the rented cabin for the party, deep in the mountains, there was no cellphone coverage.

I was able to forget about Stan for the day. The party guests enjoyed a lovely afternoon canoeing down the Russian River, then prepared a feast back at the cabin that evening. By the time I laid down to sleep, though, Stan's lack of contact started to drive me crazy.

During a sleepless night, I convinced myself that Stan was a conman. That he had somehow hacked into the bank's records to get all of my information and was thrilled that I made it so easy for him to get a $25,000 wire transfer and disappear. He was so eager to take the deal. So quick to send whatever letter I asked for. He couldn't do the telephone transfer and never appeared again once the money was sent. I'd been scammed. And with the $25,000 lost, I would be unable to settle my debts and would have to file bankruptcy.

I had to call Yellow Bank to see if my payment went in, but it was barely 3 a.m. I was up at 5 a.m. on the dot to call their East Coast customer-service number, but I couldn't get any coverage on my cellphone. I searched the cabin for a house phone, only to learn that it wouldn't allow outgoing long-distance calls. I realized that I had an 800 number for the bank and happily discovered the house phone would allow calls to 800 numbers. I reached someone at Yellow Bank who confirmed that the company Stan claimed to be from was, in fact, a collection company working for them, though the person I was on the phone with could not identify Stan by name and showed no record of my $25,000 payment or settlement agreement. Although the bank had confirmed the name of the company, I still was not convinced that some conman couldn't have gotten that information at the same time he got all of my personal information.

As soon as I returned to town and had Internet access, I found a website for the collection company. It was a legitimate financial-management services company, and the address they listed in New York was the same that Stan had given me, though the phone number was different and Stan's name was nowhere to be found among the list of employee profiles on the site. As my paranoia grew, I became more convinced that I'd been taken in and had lost $25,000.

Then I thought to check my online banking site for that account. During the entire eight months that the account was past due, it continued to list each unmade payment and the new balance on the account. Now, there was no listing at all. The account was gone from the bank's website. It didn't list the payment having been made nor did it say that there was zero due on the account. Nothing. No information. Just gone. I didn't know if that was a good thing or a bad thing. I couldn't tell if it was gone because they'd finally closed off my access to the account, but that the money was still owed, or if it was gone because they considered the account paid and closed.

I never heard from Stan again and sat in the space of not knowing for a *month* until I received a call from a different person at "Recovery Services" saying that they were calling to collect my $51,000 debt to Yellow Bank.

Hold on, bucko.

The first thing I felt, actually, was not shock that they were still trying to collect on the balance. My first feeling was relief that my $25,000 was actually received and credited to my account. Then I got upset that they hadn't processed it properly. I explained that the payment was part of a settlement agreement that I had made with Stan to pay off the account in full. I was told that Stan didn't work there anymore, and according to their records, I still owed $51,000.

Here is why having the settlement agreement in writing is so important, why I was so pleased that I had insisted on it in every conversation I'd had, including to the point of allowing one settlement to fall through. I was able to fax them the letter confirming that the payment was for full settlement. I had officially settled the first chunk of my debt.

WORKSHEET: **"THE MONEY ANGEL"**

➤ Go ahead, forward a couple of chain mails promising riches. They can't hurt.

➤ I know I said this in the last worksheet, but it's worth stressing again. ALWAYS get the settlement agreement in writing BEFORE sending in any payment.

➤ You may hear from attorneys or others that you can have ten to fifteen business days to send in a payment, but in my experience, it was all due within one to two days.

➤ Make settlement payments that are traceable. Bank wire transfers, phone transfers with a bank representative on the line, cashier's checks, or money orders sent by a delivery service with a tracking number, and KEEP the documentation.

➤ Try not to drive yourself as crazy as I did. ☺

Chapter 6

THE WILD RIDE

I'M NOT THE FIRST PERSON to observe that life is like a roller coaster. The similarity has been observed so many times that it's a cliché, though so utterly appropriate that it is hard to ignore. I could spend an hour trying to come up with a more original metaphor for the ups and downs of life experiences, waves, broken shock absorbers, hot air balloons, trampolines, whatever, but none does the job quite so well as the image of a roller coaster, up and down, slow at times, fast at times, your heart pumping then settling then pumping again.

The same week that I successfully settled my first credit card, I was served with my first lawsuit. As promised, Brown Bank had filed a complaint in Los Angeles Superior Court suing me for the $22,000 balance on the personal card account (which, I had been warned, was in "pre-legal"). I was served at home. A man came to my front gate. My dog went out to greet him. He asked my name then handed me the complaint. This would be the part of the roller-coaster ride where your stomach feels like it's been left half a mile behind you.

For your edification, since it is a document of public record, I present here the entire complaint as delivered to me, Document 4. (You may note that many of the stamped dates on the suit are in July. I did not receive the complaint until mid-August. I do not know if this is because the bank waited after filing to serve me or if it took that long for the service to arrive.)

Kenneth Golde

June 26, 2008

RE: N.A. Account No(s).

Balance: $22,381.09

Dear Kenneth Golde:

Due to your failure to pay the balance due on your account, we have been instructed to file suit against you. Additionally, as required by law, you are hereby notified that a negative credit report reflecting your credit record may be submitted to a credit reporting agency if you fail to fulfill the terms of your credit obligations.

Once a judgment is obtained, your income may be garnished and other personal property subject to levy may be seized to satisfy the judgment. If you own real property, liens could be placed thereon.

In addition to the $22,381.09 due on your account, the judgment may include costs of suit, interest and attorneys fees at the discretion of the court. You are hereby notified that, if the balance due on your account is less than $5,000.00, we opt not to use the small claims court and you could be liable for additional amounts of up to the costs of suit and, when allowed by law, attorneys' fees. Judgments can remain in your record for 10 years or longer.

Filing of the lawsuit is unavoidable. However, to avoid the unnecessary progression of the lawsuit to judgment and eventually wage garnishment, please contact one of my legal assistants immediately for repayment options at the number indicated above upon receipt of this letter. Thank you for your attention to this matter.

Very truly yours,

Document 4: The Lawsuit (this and the next several pages)

cp8 8\8\08   SUMMONS
              (CITACION JUDICIAL)

NOTICE TO DEFENDANT:
(AVISO AL DEMANDADO):
Kenneth Golde, AND DOES 1 TO 10

FOR COURT USE ONLY
(SOLO PARA USO DE LA CORTE)
CONFORMED COPY
OF ORIGINAL FILED
Los Angeles Superior Court

JUL 2 2 2008

John A. Clarke, Executive Officer/Clerk
by _____ Deputy

YOU ARE BEING SUED BY PLAINTIFF:
(LO ESTA DEMANDANDO EL DEMANDANTE).
N.A., a corporation

You have **30 CALENDAR DAYS** after this summons and legal papers are served on you to file a written response at this court and have a copy served on the plaintiff. A letter or phone call will not protect you. Your written response must be in proper legal form if you want the court to hear your case. There may be a court form that you can use for your response. You can find these court forms and more information at the California Courts Online Self-Help Center (www.courtinfo.ca.gov/selfhelp), your county law library, or the courthouse nearest you. If you cannot pay the filing fee, ask the court clerk for a fee waiver form. If you do not file your response on time, you may lose the case by default, and your wages, money, and property may be taken without further warning from the court.
There are other legal requirements. You may want to call an attorney right away. If you do not know an attorney, you may want to call an attorney referral service. If you cannot afford an attorney, you may be eligible for free legal services from a nonprofit legal services program. You can locate these nonprofit groups at the California Legal Services Web site (www.lawhelpcalifornia.org), the California Courts Online Self-Help Center (www.courtinfo.ca.gov/selfhelp), or by contacting your local court or county bar association.

Tiene 30 DIAS DE CALENDARIO después de que le entreguen esta citación y papeles legales para presentar una respuesta por escrito en esta corte y hacer que se entregue una copia al demandante. Una carta o una llamada telefónica no le protegen. Su respuesta por escrito tiene que estar en formato legal correcto si desea que procesen su caso en la corte. Es posible que haya un formulario que usted [pueda usar para su respuesta. Puede encontrar estos formularios de la corte y más información en el Centro de Ayuda de las Cortes de California (www.courtinfo.ca.gov/selfhelp/espanol), en la biblioteca de leyes de su condado o en la corte que le quede más cerca. Si no puede pagar la cuota de presentación, pida al secretario de la corte que le dé un formulario de exención de pago de cuotas. Si no presenta su repuesta a tiempo, pueda perder el caso por incumplimiento y la corte le podrá quitar su sueldo, dinero y bienes sin mas advertencia. Hay otros requisitos legales. Es recomendable que llame a un abogado inmediatamente. Si no conoce a un abogado, pueda llamar a un servicio de remisión a abogados. Si no puede pagar a un abogado, es posible que cumpla con los requisitos para obtener servicios legales gratuitos de un programa de servicios legales sin fines de lucro. Puede encontrar estos grupos sin fines de lucro en el sitio web de California, (www.courtinfo.ca.gov/selfhelp/espanol) o poniéndose en contacto con la corte o el colegio de abogados locales.

The name and address of the court is *(El nombre y dirección de la corte es)*	CASE NUMBER: *(Número del Caso)*
Superior Court Of California	#

The name, address, and telephone number of plaintiff's attorney, or plaintiff without an attorney, is:
(El nombre, la dirección y el número de teléfono del abogado del demandante, o del demandante

DATE: _____ Clerk, by _____ , Deputy
(Fecha)   *(Actuario)*   *(Delegado)*

(For proof of service of this summons, use Proof of Service of Summons (form POS-010).)
(Para prueba de entrega de esta citation use el formulario Proof of Service of Summons, (POS-010)).
NOTICE TO THE PERSON SERVED: You are served
1. ☑ as an individual defendant.
2. ☐ as the person sued under the fictitious name of *(specify):*
3. ☐ on behalf of *(specify):*

[SEAL]

    under ☐ CCP 416.10(corporation)   ☐ CCP 416.60(minor)
           ☐ CCP 416.20(defunct corporation) ☐ CCP 416.70(conservatee)
           ☐ CCP 416.40(association or partnership) ☐ CCP 416.90(individual)
           ☐ other:

4. ☐ by personal delivery on *(date):*

Form Adopted by Rule 982   (See reverse for proof of Service)   CCP 412.20
Judicial Council of California
SUM-100 [Rev. January 1, 2004]   **SUMMONS**   2001 © American LegalNet, Inc.

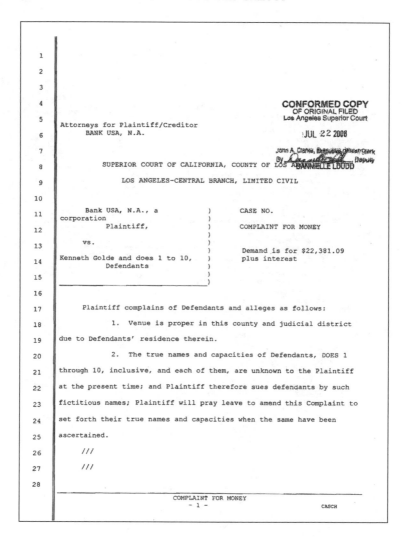

3. Plaintiff is a national banking corporation, chartered
under the laws of the United States of America with a principal place
of business at   Wilmington, Delaware.
    4. The within action is not subject to the provisions of
Section 2981, et seq. (Rees-Levering Act or Section 1801, et seq.
(Unruh Act)) of the Civil Code of the State of California.
    5. Paragraphs 1 through 4 are incorporated by reference
in each cause of action alleged hereafter as though fully re-alleged
therein.

    FIRST CAUSE OF ACTION FOR BREACH OF CONTRACT ACCOUNT NUMBER

    6 On or about   09-01-96 , Defendants applied for and
requested a Credit Card from Plaintiff,   Bank USA, N.A., a
corporation. In response to the request, Plaintiff issued a credit
card, Account Number   to Defendants. The credit
card and Credit Agreement setting forth the terms, conditions and
regulations of Plaintiff's credit facilities, including the use of a
credit card, were delivered to Defendant(s).

    7 Pursuant to the terms of the Credit Agreement,
Defendant became liable for amounts charged on the account, when
Plaintiff was notified of such charges. Plaintiff has been notified of
charges on the Credit Card and has sent to Defendant monthly
statements reflecting all charges, credits, interest accrued, fees and
payments. A procedure for disputing charges is stated in the Credit
Agreement and is also stated in Statements sent to KENNETH GOLDE. To
date, no disputes are unresolved on Account no.

    8 Among the several terms, conditions and regulations of
that credit agreement, Defendant(s) were to pay minimum payments

COMPLAINT FOR MONEY
- 2 -   CASCH

1 toward the balance of charges made with the credit privileges extended

2 to them promptly upon receipt of a monthly statement.

3   9 Defendants accepted and used their credit card and

4 incurred charges in the sum of $ 22381.09 by the use of such credit

5 card. On or about   04-15-08, Plaintiff rendered Defendants a

6 monthly statement requesting a minimum payment toward such sum,

7 pursuant to the above-mentioned credit agreement. Defendant defaulted

8 and thereby breached the agreement when Defendant failed to pay the

9 minimum monthly payment when due. Plaintiff has therefore declared

10 the entire balance owing due and payable.

11   10 That although demand for said sum has been made,

12 Defendants, and each of them, have failed, refused and neglected to

13 pay said sum. There is now due, owing and unpaid, the sum of $

14 22381.09, plus pre-judgment interest at the contract rate of 24.0% per

15 annum from and after   04-15-08.

16   11 Plaintiff has duly performed everything on its part to

17 be performed under the terms of the above-mentioned credit agreement.

18   12 The agreement between the parties provides for

19 recovery of reasonable attorney's fees and costs, in an amount to be

20 determined by the Court, if litigation becomes necessary to enforce

21 the terms of the agreement.

22   SECOND CAUSE OF ACTION FOR OPEN BOOK ACCOUNT ACCOUNT NUMBER

23

24   13 Plaintiff hereby incorporates each and every

25 allegation as contained in each paragraph of the preceding cause of

26 action as though fully set forth at length.

27   14 That within four years last past Defendants, and each

28 of them, became indebted to Plaintiff on an open book account, for a

COMPLAINT FOR MONEY
- 3 -
CASCH

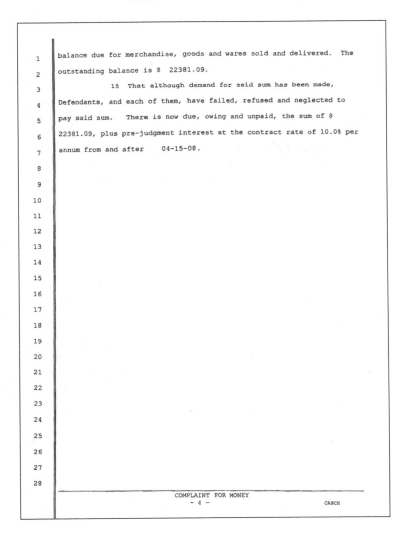

1 balance due for merchandise, goods and wares sold and delivered. The

2 outstanding balance is $ 22381.09.

3   15 That although demand for said sum has been made,

4 Defendants, and each of them, have failed, refused and neglected to

5 pay said sum.   There is now due, owing and unpaid, the sum of $

6 22381.09, plus pre-judgment interest at the contract rate of 10.0% per

7 annum from and after   04-15-08.

8

9

10

11

12

13

14

15

16

17

18

19

20

21

22

23

24

25

26

27

28

1   WHEREFORE, Plaintiff prays for judgment against the Defendants

2   and each of them, as follows:

3   As to the First Cause of Action on Account

4   the principal sum of $ 22381.09, plus pre-judgment interest thereon

5   at the contract rate of 24.0% per annum from and after   04-15-08;

6

7   As to the Second Cause of Action on Account

8   the principal sum of $ 22381.09, plus pre-judgment interest thereon

9   at the legal rate of 10.0% per annum from and after   04-15-08;

10

11

12

13

14

15

16

17

18

19

20

21

22

23

24

25

26

27

28

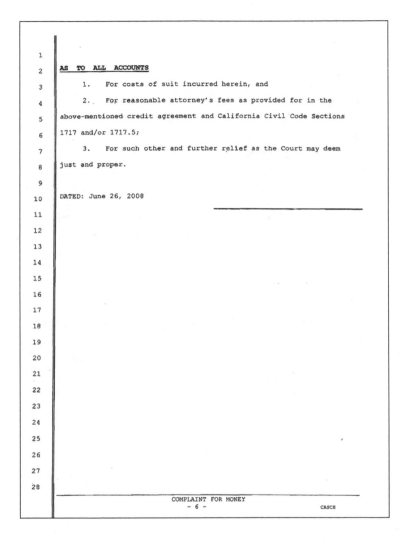

AS TO ALL ACCOUNTS

  1.   For costs of suit incurred herein, and

  2.   For reasonable attorney's fees as provided for in the
above-mentioned credit agreement and California Civil Code Sections
1717 and/or 1717.5;

  3.   For such other and further relief as the Court may deem
just and proper.

DATED: June 26, 2008

                              COMPLAINT FOR MONEY
                                  - 6 -   CASCH

1

2   <u>VERIFICATION</u>

3

4 I,

5

6   I am an Assistant Treasurer and Officer of Plaintiff

7 Bank, USA, N.A., a Corporation in the above-entitled action. I

8 am duly authorized by said corporation to make this Verification

9 on its behalf, and I make this verification for that reason. I

10 am informed and believe and on that ground, allege that the

11 matters stated in the foregoing COMPLAINT FOR MONEY are true.

12   I,   declare under penalty of perjury under

13 the laws of the State of California that the foregoing is true and

14 correct.

15

16   Executed on _____ JUL 0 2 2008 _____ at San Antonio, Texas.

17

18

19   _____

20

21

22

23

24

25

LOS ANGELES SUPERIOR COURT
CIVIL ALTERNATIVE DISPUTE RESOLUTION (ADR) PROGRAMS
[CRC 3.221 Information about Alternative Dispute Resolution]

The plaintiff shall serve a copy of the ADR Information package on each defendant along with the complaint.

ADR PROGRAMS

"Alternative Dispute Resolution (ADR)" is the term used to describe all the other options available for settling a dispute which once had to be settled in court. ADR processes such as arbitration, mediation, early neutral evaluation (ENE), and settlement conferences, are less formal than court and provide opportunities for litigants to reach an agreement using a problem-solving approach rather than the more adversarial approach of litigation.

MEDIATION A neutral third party called a "mediator" helps participants in the dispute create their own resolution. The mediator helps facilitate a discussion in which the parties reach a mutually agreed upon settlement. Therefore, mediation allows for more creative resolutions to disputes than other ADR processes.

The Court Mediation Program is governed by Code of Civil Procedure sections 1775-1775.15, California Rules of Court, Rules 3.850-3.868 and 3.870-3.878; Evidence Code sections 1115-1128, and Los Angeles Superior Court Rules, Chapter 12.

ARBITRATION A neutral third party called an "arbitrator" listens to each side in the dispute present its case. The arbitrator, who is an attorney, issues a decision based on the evidence. Although evidence is presented, arbitration is a less formal process than litigation. The decision is non-binding unless the parties agree in writing to binding arbitration.

The Court Arbitration Program is governed by Code of Civil Procedure sections 1141.10-1141.31, California Rules of Court, Rules 3.810-3.830, and Los Angeles Superior Court Rules, Chapter 12.

ENE A neutral third party called an "evaluator" will provide the parties and their counsel, on a voluntary basis and in a confidential session, the opportunity to make summary presentations of their claims and defenses, including key evidence. After hearing the presentations, the evaluator, who is an experienced lawyer with subject-matter expertise, offers a non-binding evaluation.

The evaluator will also help clarify, narrow or eliminate issues, identify areas of agreement, offer case-planning suggestions, and, if requested by parties, settlement assistance. Although settlement is not the primary goal of ENE, the ENE process can reduce litigation time and costs and promote settlement.

The Court ENE Program is governed by Los Angeles Superior Court Rules, Chapter 12.

SETTLEMENT A neutral third party called a "settlement officer," who is also a retired judge, assists the parties in
CONFERENCE negotiating their own settlement and may evaluate the strengths and weaknesses of the case.

JURISDICTIONAL LIMITATIONS

MEDIATION, Any case in which the amount in dispute is between $25,000-$50,000 per plaintiff, and was not previously
ARBITRATION referred to the Court ADR Program for mediation, arbitration, or
& ENE by stipulation, election by plaintiff or order of the court.
ENE

Parties may *voluntarily* request or initiate a mediation or arbitration proceeding, regardless of the amount in dispute.

SETTLEMENT Any case, regardless of the amount in dispute, may be ordered to a settlement conference. There is no
CONFERENCE monetary limit.

REFERRAL INFORMATION

After the Court determines the suitability of a case for ADR, the Court directs the parties to the ADR Department to initiate the ADR process. Once the parties have completed the ADR intake forms, a Neutral may be selected.

ADR 005 10-03
LASC Approved
(Rev. 01-07)

Page 1 of 2

NEUTRAL SELECTION

Parties may select a mediator or arbitrator from the Court Party Pay Panel or Pro Bono Panel or may hire someone privately, at their discretion. Parties are assigned to a settlement officer by court staff.

COURT ADR PANELS

PARTY PAY PANEL

The Party Pay Panel consists of mediators and arbitrators who have achieved a specified level of experience in court-connected cases. The parties (collectively) may be charged $150.00 per hour for the first three hours of hearing time. Thereafter, the parties may be charged for additional hearing time on an hourly basis at rates established by the mediator or arbitrator if the parties consent in writing.

PRO BONO PANEL

The Pro Bono Panel consists of trained mediators and arbitrators who have not yet gained the experience to qualify for the Party Pay Panel and experienced mediators and arbitrators who make themselves available pro bono. Mediators and arbitrators donate their time to the courts as a way of supporting the judicial system. It is the policy of the Court that all pro bono volunteer mediators and arbitrators provide three hours hearing time per case. Thereafter, the parties may be charged for additional hearing time on an hourly basis at rates established by the mediator or arbitrator if the parties consent in writing.

ENE

The Court ENE Panel consists of experienced lawyers who have been trained to serve as neutral evaluators. The evaluators provide preparation time and three hours hearing time per case at no charge. Thereafter, the parties may be charged for additional hearing time on an hourly basis at rates established by the evaluator if the parties consent in writing.

PRIVATE NEUTRAL

The market rate for private neutrals can range from $200-$1,000 per hour.

For additional information, visit the Court ADR web application at **www.lasuperiorcourt.org** (click on ADR).

Partially Funded by the Los Angeles County Dispute Resolution Program

NAME, ADDRESS, AND TELEPHONE NUMBER OF ATTORNEY OR PARTY WITHOUT ATTORNEY: | STATE BAR NUMBER | Reserved for Clerk's File Stamp

ATTORNEY FOR (Name):

SUPERIOR COURT OF CALIFORNIA, COUNTY OF LOS ANGELES

COURTHOUSE ADDRESS:

PLAINTIFF:

DEFENDANT:

**STIPULATION TO PARTICIPATE IN
ALTERNATIVE DISPUTE RESOLUTION (ADR)**

CASE NUMBER:

The undersigned parties stipulate to participate in an Alternative Dispute Resolution (ADR) process in the above-entitled action, as follows:

☐ Mediation

☐ Non-Binding Arbitration

☐ Binding Arbitration

☐ Early Neutral Evaluation

☐ Settlement Conference

☐ Other ADR Process *(describe)*: _____

Dated: _____

Name of Stipulating Party
☐ Plaintiff ☐ Defendant ☐ Cross-defendant | Name of Party or Attorney Executing Stipulation | Signature of Party or Attorney

---

Name of Stipulating Party
☐ Plaintiff ☐ Defendant ☐ Cross-defendant | Name of Party or Attorney Executing Stipulation | Signature of Party or Attorney

---

Name of Stipulating Party
☐ Plaintiff ☐ Defendant ☐ Cross-defendant | Name of Party or Attorney Executing Stipulation | Signature of Party or Attorney

---

Name of Stipulating Party
☐ Plaintiff ☐ Defendant ☐ Cross-defendant | Name of Party or Attorney Executing Stipulation | Signature of Party or Attorney

☐ Additional signature(s) on reverse

ADR 001 10-04
LASC Approved
(Rev. 01-07)

**STIPULATION TO PARTICIPATE IN
ALTERNATIVE DISPUTE RESOLUTION (ADR)**

Cal. Rules of Court, rule 3.221
Page 1 of 2

What is the goal of mediation?

The goal is to assist the parties in reaching a mutually acceptable agreement or understanding on some or all of the issues. The parties jointly become the primary decision maker in how to resolve the issues as opposed to the traditional judge and/or jury system.

Do I need an attorney for this?

While it is recommended to have an attorney and/or receive legal advice before the mediation starts, you are not required to have representation. If you do have an attorney, they may participate in the mediation with you.

How long does it take?

Face-to-face mediations generally last one to three hours. Telephone conciliations, in which the parties do not meet face to face, vary from a few days to several weeks. Much depends on the number of parties involved and the complexities of the issues. When the mediation takes place depends on parties scheduling availability.

A Mediator helps parties. . .	A Mediator does not...
♦ Have productive discussions ♦ Avoid or break impasses ♦ Defuse controversy ♦ Generate options that have potential for mutual gain ♦ Better understand each other's concerns and goals ♦ Focus on their interests rather than their positions	♦ Provide advice or opinions ♦ Offer legal information ♦ Make decisions for parties ♦ Represent or advocate for either side ♦ Judge or evaluate anyone or anything ♦ Conduct research ♦ "Take Sides"

What does it cost?

The first three hours of any mediation are free. Thereafter, charges are based on income or revenue. All fees are waived for low-income individuals.

What is the difference between the contractors listed and the Superior Court ADR Office?

The services offered by the contractors listed may be accessed immediately. Those offered by the Superior Court ADR Office, also a DRPA contractor, may not be accessed by parties until a court appearance, or at the directive of the judge assigned to the case.

Legal Advice/Information

If you want to retain an attorney, a list of state certified referral services is at courtinfo.ca.gov which also has an on-line self help legal center.

Self-Help Legal Access Centers are at the Inglewood, Palmdale, Pomona, and Van Nuys courthouses. nls-la.org and lafla.org

Court Personnel can answer non-legal questions (forms, fees, fee waivers). lasuperiorcourt.org

Low-income individuals may qualify for help from non-profit legal organizations. Court Personnel and DRPA contractors have such listings.

Dispute Resolution Programs Act (DRPA) Grants Administration Office
(213) 738-2621
(The DRP Office is not a Superior Court Office. Consult your phone directory to locate the number of the Court Office on your summons.)

THIS IS A TWO-SIDED DOCUMENT.

ADR 007 07-04
LASC Approved

Page 2 of 2

I'd never been sued before. The whole idea of it caused the feelings of self-judgment to return. I read the complaint carefully. It stated repeatedly that I owed the money. Frankly, it seemed like a lot of paper to keep saying the same thing over and over again—that I owed the money. I found it interesting that one portion said the balance due would continue accruing interest at 10 percent per annum, which was a lower interest rate, now that the account had gone into legal action, than they were charging on my card when it was current. The account was actually accruing less interest now that I was being sued.

Also interesting were the several pages at the end of the document concerning the process of mediation and arbitration.

I instantly realized something. The earlier threats that once a lawsuit was filed I would no longer be able to negotiate were *not true*. The lawsuit, like the escalating language on phone calls, was just another tool in their box aimed at getting me to settle at the highest rate possible. Of course, that insight didn't ease my anxiety while holding the complaint in my hand.

According to the complaint, I had thirty days to file a response. I consulted with my attorney, as well as several attorney friends, including my father, and learned that I didn't really have a leg to stand on in the suit. The fact that it was "verified" meant, as I understood it, that I couldn't deny that I owed the money. In many lawsuits for money, the defendant might, indeed, claim that the plaintiff is wrong and not owed the money being demanded. In my case, I had taken the loan and was definitely not repaying it as agreed to in my card application.

Past that there wasn't much clarity coming my way on how a suit of this kind might progress. What's the old saying? "If you want a different opinion, ask a different attorney."

One opinion I received was that the bank could get a very quick judgment against me, perhaps even a summary judgment, which meant it wouldn't even go to trial. With such a judgment, one attorney felt they would be able to go right into my bank accounts and take out the full amount that I owed them, plus all legal fees. Another attorney felt that even with a summary judgment, it might take months for them to get the approval to remove cash from my bank accounts, and in that time, I would keep living on that cash until there was nothing for them to claim anyway. So the judgment wouldn't amount to anything tangible.

I asked if I should remove my cash from my account and keep it at home, which would make it hard to pay my bills, but not as hard as not having the money. I was told "not yet." That wasn't too comforting as it didn't really tell me when the right time would be.

I asked about my invested money (some of my personal savings were still in the form of stocks). Could they get into my brokerage account, liquidate my stocks, and take the money from there? Yes, but that was "harder," with no explanation of how hard or what made it harder or how they could do it. I did learn that they would not be able to take money from my Roth IRA. Retirement accounts are judgment proof. I transferred $5,000 into my Roth. That was a hard decision, as I knew I might need that money to buy down debt or live on, but I felt it was better to protect it in the event of a judgment.

The topic of bankruptcy resurfaced. Bankruptcy would stop the lawsuit, prevent any judgment, prevent any attaching of wages, taking of cash from my accounts, or attaching a lien on my home. Though, as previously discussed, bankruptcy would also put me into financial receivership where my cash, stocks, and car would be turned over to pay off my creditors. I wasn't ready for that step yet, but was prepared to take it if the lawsuit progressed to judgment.

One good thing about the suit going to the legal department (by the way, it did not go to an outside firm but to Brown Bank's in-house legal department) was that they would now speak to my attorney, whereas the regular "loss prevention" department never would. On my behalf, my attorney offered them the same $7,000 that I was always prepared to pay. I did not hear from him that they had made any response. A couple of weeks passed, and I was getting nervous about the thirty-day deadline to prepare a response to the case. I didn't even know what kind of a response to prepare. As I said, I couldn't deny the debt, the most I could do was to give the "story" of how I'd gotten there and perhaps, according to my attorney, dispute the interest that they had added to my balance, as they had done those calculations, not me.

I was quite surprised when someone from the Brown Bank collection department called me on the same account for which I was being sued. I'd been unable to get anyone at the bank itself on the phone for this account since the awkward day when I'd offered $12,000 thinking it was the business card with the $39,000 balance. Once I'd received the complaint, whenever I called on this account, I was told it had gone to legal and that the agent on the phone did not know how to transfer me.

My initial surprise quickly gave way to an insight. They still wanted to negotiate. I told the agent that my attorney had made a settlement offer of $7,000. I expected them to come back with $10,000, which they had offered long ago on this account. This time, they countered $16,000! There's a strategy, reverse negotiating. I couldn't do it, not even an option. Settling at $16,000, which was more than 60 percent, would leave me only $4,000 (of the $45,000 I had received to settle the debt), with the other $39,000 card still out there. Settling that account for 10 percent when the same bank was now suing me because I wouldn't accept 50 percent seemed unlikely.

I scheduled a meeting with my attorney to prepare the response to the complaint and to discuss filing bankruptcy if the suit progressed. After the excitement of settling with Yellow Bank, the possibility that I would have to file bankruptcy anyway was depressing.

My attorney's office is in West Los Angeles. I drove in from Hollywood early to have lunch before meeting with him. I was in a Vietnamese restaurant having noodle soup when Brown Bank called me again. As before, I offered the $7,000. This agent came down from the ridiculous $16,000 of the last call to the $10,000 that had been offered two months ago. Back then I had refused, but now I was on my way to the attorney to discuss bankruptcy again. Although I recognized the lawsuit as just a new tool from the box to get me to settle at the best possible rate for them, it worked. I accepted the $10,000.

Once again, the agent seemed surprised and eager. He asked me to hold while he checked in with the gatekeeper. Sitting on hold, eating my noodle soup, wouldn't you know it — my cell phone cut out. This is the bank with no extensions, where I can never call back the same person who called me. I couldn't even get anyone to talk to me about this account when I called because it had been charged off to legal. A few moments later he called back — the same person — and said that the $10,000 had been approved. I asked for a letter confirming the settlement agreement. This was the same bank that had once promised me a letter that finally arrived pre-dated. I made it clear that I was heading to my attorney's office, gave his fax number, and said that if they faxed through an acceptable letter within the next hour, I'd be able to get a cashier's check today, and they would have it the next morning. He said he'd do it.

I went to my attorney's office and filled him in. He looked at me with disapproval. He told me that they had come back to him with $10,000 already and that he had countered at $8,500 and was waiting to hear on that. He'd never told me that. No wonder they jumped at my offer of $10,000 this time. Again, evidence for exactly why they called me directly. My lawyer was doing a better job of negotiating for me, and they were able to catch me in fear and anxiety and get a better settlement by going around him. Just as I had the feeling after settling with Yellow Bank for $25,000, I felt now that I might have done better if I'd actually let the lawsuit move forward.

Admittedly, however, I didn't have the stomach to see it that far to save fifteen hundred dollars. However, I wasn't certain of this deal yet. The last "agreement" I had with Brown Bank came with a bogus letter. My attorney and I made idle chit chat, not really wanting to have a detailed conversation about preparing my response to the lawsuit if the suit was about to be settled. I was shocked when the letter actually came through. (See Document 5.)

August 21, 2008

Kenneth Golde

RE: **Bank USA, N.A. vs. Kenneth Golde**
             Case No.:
             Account No.:

Dear KENNETH GOLDE:

    This letter shall serve to confirm that   Bank USA, N.A. shall accept $ **10,000.00** as settlement in full of the above-referenced matter. This amount shall be due as set forth in the attached payment schedule.

    Payment can be called in to our Litigation Support Division at 800   or can be mailed to Bank USA, N.A. at the above address. It will take 30 days after the check is posted to the account for a DISMISSAL REQUEST or SATISFACTION OF JUDGMENT to be generated.

    After you have reviewed this letter agreement, please date and countersign in the area indicated below and return this letter in the enclosed self-addressed, stamped envelope.

    If there are any further questions, please contact me at **213**

                            Very truly yours,

                            Attorneys for Plaintiff/Creditor
                            Bank USA, N.A.

    I have read and consent and agree to the terms of this letter with the attached payment schedule.

DATED: _8/21/08_   _____
                            Kenneth Golde

Document 5: Second legitimate settlement letter, ending the
lawsuit with Brown Bank on my personal account

My attorney called to confirm the letter directly with the legal department. We got a lawyer on the phone (not just one of the call-center agents), and it was confirmed. We asked if they wanted a cashier's check or wire transfer. It was past 2 p.m., and I wouldn't be able to do a wire transfer until the next day. The lawyer we were speaking to couldn't answer as to the best method for making the payment. Apparently, the attorney directly responsible for my account, who had approved the $10,000 when the guy on the phone put me on hold an hour ago, was now not in the office to answer that question. We left word for him to call me directly with his preference. But not wanting to wait, I went to the bank, got the cashier's check, and took it to FedEx.

I was feeling pretty good. I had spent $35,000 and settled $98,000 of my debt, which was now reduced to $114,000, from the original $212,000.

Driving home, I received a call from the attorney on my account. It was the first time I had spoken to him directly. I told him that I'd over-nighted a cashier's check and gave him the tracking number. He said that was acceptable and then asked me how I was handling the situation of my debt. The way he asked it was different from all the other collections conversations I'd had. He and I had just reached a settlement that he was pleased with, and the question was not only friendly, but personable. I answered honestly that it had been a difficult year, but that I felt good about starting to work through the debt. He seemed appreciative of my situation and admitted that his desk was fuller than it had ever been with people in situations just like mine.

As the call wound to an end, he said, "We really hope that you sell your film, get liquid again, have future projects, and that you'll come to us for your banking and borrowing needs." Here I had just settled a $22,000 debt for $10,000 and not an hour later the attorney who was suing me on behalf of the bank was expressing an eagerness to do business with me again.

Several weeks later I received the official court documents dismissing the case. I particularly like the sentence, "No balance remains due and owing." (See Documents 6a and 6b, below.)

November 14, 2008

Kenneth Golde

RE: Bank   N.A. vs. Kenneth Golde
             CASE NO.
             ACCOUNT NO.

Dear Kenneth Golde:

     Pursuant to your request,   Bank   N.A., hereby acknowledges receipt of settlement in full of the above matter. No balance remains due and owing.

     A copy of the Dismissal/Satisfaction of Judgment sent to court is enclosed herein for your records.

     A conformed copy may be obtained from the Court once it has been entered.

Document 6a: Letter from Brown Bank confirming dismissal of the lawsuit.

Document 6b. Copy of the "Request for Dismissal" submitted to the court

As much as I hated receiving that first lawsuit, I found myself hoping that the collection agent who was holding the $39,000 account at this same bank would refer it to legal, that I would get sued and be able to deal with this same lawyer in the settlement. I felt confident that he would honor the original $13,656 offer that the bank had made with me on that account.

The roller coaster was racing along. I was actually excited about the prospect of settling more accounts and felt that I was getting better at the process.

So much so that when I received a call from a new collections agent representing Blue Bank, I didn't experience any of the heart flutter that had come previously. I had a sense of knowing where this could lead and was prepared for it. I didn't flinch when he said my account was in "pre-legal," as I now knew that insinuating a lawsuit was just another ploy to induce me to make a payment.

The agent called himself "Mr. Stone." I have heard that the names many collection agents use are not their real names. I once knew a man who was a collection agent, and he told me that he had filed a fictitious business name that was a real name, like "John Diamond." All of his phone calls and correspondence to the people he was trying to collect from were in the name "John Diamond." It was the name of his business, so to speak. So I had some doubt that Mr. Stone was actually Mr. Stone. In any case, he called about the $21,000 account that was by that time six months past due at Blue Bank. He said sternly, "This account is in pre-legal and that means that you are entering an entirely different situation than you've ever been in before."

Oh, but I wasn't. I'd been in this territory before. I'd been in pre-legal, I'd been past pre-legal. I remained calm, unfazed by his intimidating tone, and told Mr. Stone that I was willing to settle. He said they couldn't settle for less than 85 percent. No surprise there. I said I had $5,000 (about 25 percent). He virtually exploded. "Why on earth would we take $5,000 on a $21,000 debt? Would you take $5,000 on a $21,000 debt? I can't think of a good reason why anyone would take $5,000 on a $21,000 debt. How did you get yourself in this position?"

I brought out the story. I entered into a business deal with a partner, we went over budget, my partner passed away leaving me with the debt, the economy turned downward, I couldn't sell the business asset, I haven't been able to sell my house, the Writer's Guild strike, the Screen Actors Guild dispute, I really would rather not be in this position.

He said, "I'll tell you what I can do. This offer is only good for forty-eight hours. [Sound familiar?] I can take $10,000."

Wow, from about $18,000 to $10,000 in less than five minutes.

"Well, Mr. Stone," I said, "I don't have the $10,000. But I have the $5,000. I can send you the five thousand today by wire transfer or cashier's check."

He wasn't ready to give in yet. "I don't care what you do, but you have to take care of this. You have to come up with $10,000 if you want this to go away before it goes into legal, and then it'll be out of my hands, and you'll be in an entirely different situation than you've ever been in before." (He actually used that same phrase, "an entirely different situation," several times during the call.)

I could have read his script back to him at this point. I had totally removed myself from the emotionality of the situation. This was a business negotiation, and it was actually kind of fun.

I told him I would take a look at my finances and see what

I could do. He reminded me that I had to call him back in two days. "I'll be happy to. Do you have an extension?" He did. That was a surprise for me. I would actually be able to speak to the same person again? "And what is your first name, Mr. Stone?"

Sternly: "That's not important."

"Not important? Why not?"

"You can call me Mr. Stone."

It was silly. I smiled to myself. "Okay, Mr. Stone."

In those two days, I looked at my finances. I felt $10,000 was too high for me. I would have nothing left of the $45,000 and be far short of my initial goal of settling $135,000 with that money. And yet I wanted to settle. I wavered, feeling the emotional tug to make the deal. Then, as if to help me make a decision, I learned that I had to put another $9,000 into my film to create several delivery elements for the foreign-sales agent. With my personal savings depleting, I knew I couldn't go to $10,000 on this account and would have to stick to my goal of $7,500.

Two days later, I called Mr. Stone. He wasn't in. His voicemail said that he would be out that day, a Friday, and the following Monday, returning on Tuesday.

On Tuesday, I called again. Mr. Stone answered with his typically stern voice, but remembering that he'd taken Friday and Monday off, I asked him, "How was your long weekend? Did you take a vacation?"

The stern voice disappeared. I heard him smile. "Why, yes I did. I went fishing with my sons."

"Fishing. That sounds wonderful. How old are your sons?"

"Eighteen and sixteen."

"Oh, that sounds great." (It really did). "Did you catch anything?"

For five minutes Mr. Stone told me about his weekend. The fish, the lake, his boys. He laughed, and I could tell he smiled. And I did, too. I was happy for him. He'd gone from cop voice to human voice, from bill collector to human being, and I don't think he even realized it.

"What a lovely story, Mr. Stone. By the way, what's your first name?"

"Tim."

"Tim. I'm so glad you had a nice weekend, Tim. I had a good weekend, too."

"Did you? What did you do?"

"Well, I looked at my finances and determined that I can come up with $1,300 more. I can offer you $6,300."

"Really?" He seemed surprised and pleased. I'm sure he got on this call expecting a battle, and instead, he was reminiscing about a great weekend with his sons and getting a better offer without having to ask for it. He didn't say, "You have to come up with $10,000." He didn't say, "You are entering an entirely different situation than you've ever been in before."

He said, "Let me submit it. I'll call you back soon." Half an hour later, Mr. Stone said that the bank would settle for $7,400. If I wanted, I could pay $6,000 today and $1,400 in a month. I chose to pay it all that day, on one condition: the settlement agreement in writing. He faxed it to me right away. I had a cashier's check made out in the name of Blue Bank sent by FedEx within the hour.

```
                                                              9/9/08

ATTN: KENNETH A GOLDE


RE:     #:                      ($21,044.84)

Dear Kenneth Golde:

This will confirm that        Bank is prepared to accept $7,400.00 on      #
                      as settlement in full of the referenced account.

Your payment of $7,400.00, in guaranteed funds, must be received, as follows:  fedex overnight on
9/9/08 for $6,300.00 down, with the remaining payment of $1,100.00, fedex overnight nlt 10/9/08.

Check Payable to:            Bank
Fedex Overnight Delivery Address:




If you have any questions, please contact me at phone#866

                                   Sincerely,



                                   Account Manager
                                   Recovery Section
```

Document 7: Third legitimate settlement letter, Blue Bank

I had now settled $119,000 in credit-card debt for only $42,400, just about 35 percent. I still had $93,000 in debt remaining and wanted to bring it down more, but I had only $2,600 left of the $45,000 intended to put toward settlements.

I began to consider using my savings to reduce more of my debt. I was down to roughly $25,000 in personal funds. It was not lost on me that, with the exception of keeping my car, it might have been more financially advantageous to have filed bankruptcy months before. I would have been able to keep $22,000 and have all my debt turned over to the "Super Creditor." Still, in my own world of emotional comparisons, I felt better about settling the debt than filing bankruptcy, and frankly, though it was a topsy-turvy ride, I was enjoying the process of negotiating settlements. It was a challenge, and I was learning from it all.

I returned my attention to my largest outstanding account, the $39,000 account with Brown Bank. It was on this account that Brown Bank had made a settlement offer of $13,656, only to delay sending me the settlement agreement until after they sent the account to collections. Then the collections company, "Management Services," refused to honor the agreement that I had reached with the bank. It had been several months since I had spoken to Brown Bank or "Management Services." In those months, late summer and fall of 2008, the bottom had completely fallen out of the banking industry. Bear Stearns, Lehman Brothers, and Washington Mutual no longer existed. Countless other banks and financial institutions, large and small, were in danger of failing. Financial markets were tumbling across the globe. Layoffs and the unemployment rate were up, stock portfolios were down, and the Treasury Department of the United States began overseeing an $850-billion bailout of U.S. banks.

I thought, with all of this going on, that Brown Bank might be more likely to settle than previously. If I could persuade them to honor the original agreement for $13,656, it would reduce my personal savings to only $14,000, but it would also reduce my debt to $54,000. I felt that would be manageable after starting at $212,000.

I called Brown Bank myself to reopen negotiations. The agent told me the account was in charge off (which I knew) and redirected me again to "Management Services."

I spoke to "Lisa" at "Management Services," explaining

the story to her and indicating that I was still willing to honor the $13,656 that Brown Bank had offered to settle the account. As I expected, she said "they" never go that low. Then she countered at $20,000.

Though I wasn't going to accept—it would leave me practically out of cash—I took the counter-offer as a good sign that they were willing to negotiate. Rather than recounter, I simply told her that $20,000 was too high. She came down instantly.

"Could you do eighteen or nineteen thousand?" she asked.

I said, "No."

She came down again. "Could you do sixteen thousand?"

"No."

"What about $15,000? You could pay the $13,500 now and the remaining $1,500 in a month."

That was interesting. Looking at the details, I noted silently that I had actually offered $13,656 (35 percent). By rounding that down to $13,500 and offering $15,000, it was only $1,344 more than my offer. The total was 38 percent of the $39,000 balance. In the lawsuit on the other Brown Bank account, I settled for $10,000 on a $22,000 balance, more than 45 percent.

While I was thinking, Lisa reminded me that if the account went into legal I would be "liable for the full balance plus legal fees" and that if there was a judgment against me they could "garnish my wages, attach my bank accounts and put a lien on my home." I had heard all that before, of course, and was not intimidated.

Not intimidated, but still a bit emotional. I remembered that I was much more anxious to settle during the lawsuit. Despite my earlier "hopes" that this account might be sent to legal, I realized in the moment that I was not so eager for that to happen. I did a little more thinking. This account had not accrued any interest since I stopped making payments eleven months earlier in December 2007. I don't know why.

As we'll see later, another account of mine was accruing interest while I wasn't making payments, and that would play a factor in my settlement. But for some reason, this account had frozen right where it was when I stopped making payments. The monthly payment at that time was approximately $950. Continuing to make my monthly payments would have been $10,450. I'm guessing that two-thirds of that would have been interest, so that my balance would still be close to $35,000 or $36,000. I would have paid more than $10,000 and still owed roughly the same amount.

Now they were offering to settle the account in full for not much more than I would have paid anyway. Though I had once hoped to settle this account for $10,000, I really did not want to go into another lawsuit, and even I had to concede that this felt like a good deal. I accepted the offer.

Unlike the difficulties I had getting a settlement letter on this account previously, the process was very smooth this time, as it had been with all the collection companies. Lisa agreed to send me a letter. It came through in half an hour.

I forwarded the letter to my attorney to review. He noted that the letter did not contain my account number and suggested that I have them resend the letter with it to protect me in the event Brown Bank attempted to collect on the balance, as Yellow Bank had done. I phoned Lisa back and asked her to resend the letter with my account number. I received it within thirty minutes, went to the bank, had a cashier's check drawn, and took it to FedEx. (See Document 8, below.)

You may note that the settlement letters I received make the particular point that the payment must be received by the due date or the agreement would be void. I made certain to either make payment by wire transfer or by cashier's check sent via FedEx. In both cases, I kept either the wire transfer document with the date or the FedEx receipt with the date as proof of sending. For FedEx, I also went online the next day to retrieve the scan of the delivery signature and printed it to add to my file.

November 17, 2008

Kenneth Golde

RE: Settlement Agreement
RMS Claim Number:

Creditor: BANK USA, N.A.
Your Current Balance: $ 39,015.30
Settlement Offer: $ 15,000.00

Dear Mr. Golde:

Management Services has authorization to accept $ 15,000.00 as a settlement in full on the above-referenced account. By completing this Settlement Agreement,   Management Services agrees to stop any further collection activity from being taken against you on this account. The settlement is contingent upon the following:

- An initial payment of $13,500.00 is due by November 18, 2008.
- One (1) final payment of $1,500.00 is due by December 12, 2008.

Upon completion of the Settlement Agreement,   Management Services will notify our customer that you have fulfilled the terms of the Settlement Agreement and our customer will then update your credit report to reflect a settled account. However, if your payment is returned for any reason or arrives after the settlement due date, this settlement offer will be considered null and void. If you have any questions, please call our offices toll free at 1-866-

Please consider this as notice that if payment is made by consumer check, we will convert this check to an electronic debit to your account via ACH and if the check is returned NSF, we will represent the check via ACH debit.

WE ARE ACTING AS A DEBT COLLECTOR. THIS LETTER IS AN ATTEMPT TO COLLECT THIS DEBT AND ANY INFORMATION OBTAINED WILL BE USED FOR THAT PURPOSE.
NOTICE: SEE REVERSE SIDE FOR IMPORTANT INFORMATION.

Please refer to   Claim number   in all communications and on all payment methods.

Sincerely,

Document 8: Fourth legitimate settlement letter, Brown Bank

The settlement letter from "Management Services" also included another document that I had not seen before either from a bank or collection company, an explanation of some of the rights I had under state and federal laws in dealing with collections agents.

IMPORTANT NOTICE OF YOUR RIGHTS UNDER FEDERAL LAW

If this is the first written notice you have received from this office in regard to the debt referred to on the other side of this letter and this is a consumer debt, then:
Unless you notify this office within 30 days after receiving this notice that you dispute the validity of this debt or any portion thereof, this office will assume this debt is valid. If you notify this office in writing within 30 days from receiving this notice that you dispute the validity of this debt or any portion thereof, this office will obtain verification of the debt or obtain a copy of a judgment, if any, and mail you a copy of such judgment or verification. If you request this office in writing within 30 days after receiving this notice this office will provide you with the name and address of the original creditor, if different from the current creditor.

WE ARE ACTING AS A DEBT COLLECTOR. THIS LETTER IS AN ATTEMPT TO COLLECT THIS DEBT AND ANY INFORMATION OBTAINED WILL BE USED FOR THAT PURPOSE.

We are required under state law to give you the following notices, some of which refer to rights you also have under federal law. This list does not contain a complete list of the rights which consumers or commercial businesses have under state and federal law. Note the following which apply in the specified states:

STATE	APPLICABLE NOTICE
California	The state Rosenthal Fair Debt Collection Practices Act and the federal Fair Debt Collection Practices Act require that, except under unusual circumstances, collectors may not contact you before 8 a.m. or after 9 p.m. They may not harass you by using threats of violence or arrest or by using obscene language. Collectors may not use false or misleading statements or call you at work if they know or have reason to know that you may not receive personal calls at work. For the most part, collectors may not tell another person, other than your attorney or spouse, about your debt. Collectors may contact another person to confirm your location or enforce a judgment. For more information about debt collection activities, you may contact the Federal Trade Commission at 1-877-FTC-HELP or www.ftc.gov.
Colorado (consumers only)	FOR INFORMATION ABOUT THE COLORADO FAIR DEBT COLLECTION PRACTICES ACT, SEE WWW.AGO.STATE.CO.US/CAB.HTM
Massachusetts	Massachusetts requires us to give the following notice, however, all consumers have these or similar rights under federal law: NOTICE OF IMPORTANT RIGHTS: YOU HAVE THE RIGHT TO MAKE A WRITTEN OR ORAL REQUEST THAT TELEPHONE CALLS REGARDING YOUR DEBT NOT BE MADE TO YOU AT YOUR PLACE OF EMPLOYMENT. ANY SUCH ORAL REQUEST WILL BE VALID FOR ONLY TEN DAYS UNLESS YOU PROVIDE WRITTEN CONFIRMATION OF THE REQUEST POSTMARKED OR DELIVERED WITHIN SEVEN DAYS OF SUCH REQUEST. YOU MAY TERMINATE THIS REQUEST BY WRITING TO THE COLLECTION AGENCY.

Document 9: Individual rights in regard to debt collectors

I am not qualified to interpret the notices presented in Document 9. However, the document directs consumers to the Federal Trade Commission (*www.ftc.gov*) for further information about debt collection activities.

Upon settling my second account with Brown Bank, my overall debt stood at $54,000, down from $212,000,

a reduction of $158,000 at a cost of $57,400. A savings of
$100,000!

I felt great that my debt had been reduced by so much
and at how much I had saved, but I was not out of the pro-
verbial woods yet. My personal savings were down to about
$12,000, barely three months of living expenses before
I would have to sell my car or reach into my IRA (which
didn't have much in it anyway and had fallen by about half
since the financial markets crashed in September 2008).

I was planning to stop settling my debt for a while anyway. *Uncross the Stars* was completely finished in October,
and I had fulfilled the delivery requirements to the foreign
distributor so that they could start making international
sales. I felt I could finally turn my attention toward finding
work.

Then Red Bank called. They had stopped calling me
months before when I told them I had a bankruptcy attorney. They never called my attorney, and he never called them
because I hadn't engaged him for this account. I'd received
periodic letters urging me to make the monthly payments
and bring my account up to date or I "could lose many of
the benefits of being a cardholder." At the time, I was fo-
cused on the other cards.

Now the account had charged off to a collection company. I had learned that the best approach for me with collection agents was to be pleasant. "How are you? I'm fine.
Yes, I'd really love to take care of this. I really don't like being
in debt. I miss my 800 FICO score."

The collection agent said the account had a balance of
roughly $23,300. That surprised me. I had done a thor-
ough inventory of all my debt when I began this process,

and had noted that my account at Red Bank had a balance of just less than $20,000. When I asked about the discrepancy, she told me that the account had been accruing interest during all the months I had not been making my monthly payments. I then realized (as mentioned earlier) that some of my accounts were accruing interest and others were not. I have no explanation for this, other that to hazard the guess that different banks have different practices. I then asked her if she could waive the interest that had accrued, but she refused.

I considered my finances. I had only $12,000 in savings. Whatever deal I made here had to be a good one, better even than any I had previously made. I offered $5,000. Immediately, the agent said, "This bank will never reduce a balance by more than $15,000. So we can take $8,300." It was her first offer. I wished I'd started at $2,000. I didn't have much wiggle room. I came back at $6,000. She declined, repeating, "This bank will never reduce a balance by more than $15,000." Then she paused and added, "Well, wait a moment. What I could do is . . . I have seen them do what's called a *below blanket settlement*."

I found that humorous. She was, effectively, saying that they have a floor they never go below except when they go below the floor, and then they even have a name for doing something they never do.

To "help me get" (she was helping me now) a *below blanket settlement*, she would have to get some financial information from me. She wanted to know my social security number, my home mortgage, was I making the mortgage payments, the estimated current value of my house, my income, what my balances were on other cards, who I was making settlements with, and of course, my whole "story" of how I'd gotten into debt and behind on payments. I'd learned before that she probably already had most, if not all, of this information at her fingertips, so I had no problem providing it to her. She said she'd call me back in a couple of days.

When she called back, she said that my offer of $6,000 was rejected on the basis that I had only one other delinquent account showing in my credit profile and that my credit score was still too high for them to approve a *below blanket settlement*. I was shocked. I had stopped making payments on five cards nearly a year ago and had now reached settlements with four of them for far less than I owed. How could it be that my credit score was still "too high"?

I hadn't bothered to check my credit score through this entire process and actually tried to convince her that my financial situation was in crisis mode. I had $12,000 to my name, $54,000 in debt, and no work prospects! She wouldn't buy it. She confirmed that they would still offer me a settlement of $15,000 less than the total balance, $9,300.

Something didn't add up. I checked my notes and confirmed that the offer had been $8,300. She told me that a billing cycle had passed while she was submitting my $6,000 offer. Interest had been added, increasing my balance to $24,600, and their settlement offer was now $9,300. The balance on this account had now increased by more than $5,000, about 25 percent, since I'd stopped making my monthly payments. She had refused a *below blanket settlement* and insisted that the best they could do was $15,000 less than the balance (pointing out that she was actually doing about $300 better than that). I realized that each month I waited, my balance and settlement price would increase. It went up by $1,300 just in this one billing cycle. Still, if I paid them $9,300 now I would be left with barely $3,000. True panic mode!

The agent heard the desperate hesitation in my voice and offered to split the settlement into three monthly payments of $3,100. It didn't exactly solve my problem, but it left me a few months cash to live on to continue pursuing the sale of the film or find a job, which I was now looking for full time. I could stretch those few thousand dollars by another month or two if I stopped making my mortgage payment, which I was loathed to do as I had managed to keep current on my mortgage thus far.

I told her that I would accept the offer if they agreed to suppress the interest from the moment we made the agreement. The agent accepted, and within twenty minutes, faxed me a settlement agreement. However, there was nothing in the agreement about suppressing the interest, as we had agreed. I called back and asked to have the language added to the agreement. The agent told me that they used standard forms that could not be amended, though she would make a note in my file that no further interest was to accrue on my account. That would not be good enough for me. I told her that I would require the language about suppressing all further interest to be in the agreement. She offered to let me speak to her supervisor, who quickly came on the line and said that she could add the language to the agreement, which I received soon afterward. (See Document 10, below.)

November 24, 2008

GOLDE, KENNY

Client: NA
Account:
Master #:
Balance: $ 24,591.34
Settlement: $9300.00

Dear Mr. Golde:

            on behalf of   will settle the above mentioned account for **$9300.00 (agreement: interest will be supressed during settlement period)** . This will release you from further obligations regarding this matter once funds have cleared.

Be advised that any settlement write-off over $800.00 (*six hundred dollars*) could be reported to the Internal Revenue Services by our client.

The above-mentioned account will be closed and returned to our client as settled in full. Our client will update this information to the credit reporting agencies.

Arrangement is: **$3100 due due November 26th, $3100 due December 29th, 2008 and $3100 due January 26th 2009.**

If you have any questions, feel free to call our office. Our office hours are Monday-Friday 6am-7pm PST.

Thank you,

Account Representative

This communication is by a debt collector. This is an attempt to collect a debt, and any information obtained will be used for that purpose.

The state Rosenthal Fair Debt Collection Practices Act and the federal Fair Debt Collection Practices Act require that, except under unusual circumstances, collectors may not contact you before 8 a.m. or after 9 p.m. They may not harass you by using threats of violence or arrest or by using obscene language. Collectors may not use false or misleading statements or call you at work if they know or have reason to know that you may not receive personal calls at work. For the most part, collectors may not tell another person, other than your attorney or spouse, about your debt. Collectors may contact another person to confirm your location or enforce a judgment. For more information about debt collection activities, you may contact the Federal Trade Commission at 1-877-FTC-HELP or www.ftc.gov

Document 10: Settlement agreement from Red Bank

This is a good time to point out another issue when it comes to settling credit-card debt. You'll notice that the second paragraph in this letter advises that any settlement write-off more than $600 could be reported to the Internal Revenue Service. I checked with my accountant on this. It is true (amazing, but true). The IRS treats debt forgiveness in this manner as income, and one could be issued a 1099 by the creditor for the forgiven amount, which becomes taxable income. That was quite a scare for me with $115,000 in total debt forgiveness. I was suddenly imagining a new $50,000 debt, not to a bank, but to the IRS. I quickly checked with my accountant and learned that because my debt was incurred as a business expense and I had business receipts, I can offset the 1099 amount with legitimate deductions. However, write-offs of debt incurred through personal expenses may be subject to taxation.[8]

Once I had made all three payments on my settlement with Red Bank, by the end of January 2009, I had successfully reduced my credit-card debt by 85 percent to $30,000. It cost me $67,000 (actually $66,700), and I saved $115,000. It took a year from when I first stopped making my monthly payments, nine months from when I first indicated to my creditors that I was interested in reaching negotiated settlements and five months from the first bank offer to this latest. Frankly, I do not see how I could have reduced my credit card debt by $182,000 in one year in any other way, short of filing bankruptcy.

---

[8] This can be a big deal. If you have questions about how settling your credit cards might affect your tax situation, consult your own tax preparer, attorney, or financial adviser.

WORKSHEET: "THE WILD RIDE"

➤ If you do receive a court summons, immediately consult your attorney. You must respond within the response period (in my case it was thirty days).

➤ A lawsuit, while applying more emotional and time pressure, does still represent another opportunity to settle.

➤ If you believe you don't have the money to make any settlement payments, do the math on your monthly payments on your current accounts. It could be that by not making the minimum payment for several months, you could save close to enough to make a settlement payment with money that you would have sent in anyway toward interest.

➤ Visit the Federal Trade Commission website, *www.ftc.gov*, for information on your rights in regard to debt collection practices.

➤ Consult your accountant regarding the implications of tax liability on forgiven debt.

Chapter 7

MANY SUCCESSES

I N JANUARY 2009, I STILL had two open accounts totaling $30,000 in credit-card debt, $17,500 to Green Bank and $12,500 to White Bank. I was staying current on those accounts for two reasons. First, I held a lingering desire to maintain some form of credit (now discarded, I use only a debit card); second, and more importantly, I had no money left to put toward settlements. Soon, the option of keeping the accounts current would not be available to me, either, as even the monthly payments on just two cards was taking a large chuck out of my nearly depleted savings that I was putting toward living expenses.

Before I delve into more hardships, I do want to take the time to acknowledge the successes in my life at that time. I feel, generally, we all spend far too much energy focusing on the negatives in our lives without giving equal (or greater) weight to the positives.

For me, the biggest win of early 2009 was this book. I originally self published *The Do-It-Yourself Bailout*, and people were finding their way to www.SettleYourCreditCards.com and buying it. I had a new focus for my days: blogging, writing and posting articles, contacting press for reviews, and counseling readers on settling their debts.

The book received a great boost of exposure from my appearance on the KCAL 9/CBS 2 News in Los Angeles. The reporter called the book "a must-read," and the coverage led to the first four hundred or so copies being sold. It also generated other press, the Thom Hartmann radio program, *Consumers Digest* magazine, AOL.com, and lots of other radio, Web, and local television.

Much as I love being a screenwriter and filmmaker, and while I have always taken pleasure in providing entertainment for people, I cannot express how fulfilling it was to be helping people the way I am through this book. The emails I received expressed that my readers felt better about themselves and their lives, how they didn't feel so alone, how they felt normal, and how they used their new position of emotional strength and health to move forward and settle their credit-card debt. Such emails were my income in those months, my own nourishment to continue facing and conquering my own financial battles. I had a new career as a public speaker and coach. I had come from the depths of despair over my debt just nine months earlier to being nearly debt free and helping others find emotional control over their finances and settle their debts, as well. Soon, I was able to say with no small amount of pride that readers of *The Do-It-Yourself Bailout* had settled more than a million dollars of their own debt. I felt it was a real testament to my commitment to "live life" even while still struggling with my financial situation.

Unfortunately, as I mentioned earlier, I was nearly broke.

While fun and fulfilling, selling *The Do-It-Yourself Bailout* was not providing me a real income. While I had visions (and still do) of being interviewed by Oprah and on

Good Morning America and reaching the fifty or so million Americans in credit-card debt who could use this book, sales were basically paying for printing, publicity, and travel for interviews. Very little found its way into my bank account.

Having spent all of my savings on settling out the first $182,000 of my credit-card debt and on living expenses for the past two years, by April 2009, I literally had $1,500 in my savings account and maybe $15,000 in my IRA, from which I'd lose 20 percent if I cashed out.

I had still not found a distributor in the United States for *Uncross the Stars*. It had sold in some foreign territories, including a nice sale to Fox Studios for all of Latin America, but the sales weren't enough to surpass the distributor's costs, so we didn't see any return. Due to the Writers Guild and potential Screen Actors Guild strikes and other factors of the economy and my personal life, I had not found new work nor received any kind of paycheck since directing *Uncross the Stars* in June of 2007 (and all of that had gone back into the costs of production and servicing the debt).

Finally, to maximize my ability to buy food and gas for the car, I stopped making payments on my last two, current credit-card accounts, even though I didn't have the money to settle. I'll admit, while I had gotten comfortable having phone calls with collection agents when I was making settlement offers, taking those calls when I just couldn't pay at all was an entirely new level of emotional doubt and fear that I hadn't previously experienced.

How could I take a call from a collection agent and just say, "I can't pay?" I found the result to be very interesting. Whereas all of the previous collection agents I'd spoken with called regularly while I was saying I had money to settle, after a few months of saying I couldn't pay at all, they stopped calling. I was very surprised. Maybe it had something to do with the economy and the vast number of people behind in their payments. Whatever the reason, I was thankful for the relief.

Even so, a little break from the collection calls wasn't going to help me in a few weeks when my last savings were gone. Many people asked me, given that I was running out of money anyway, if I felt I would have been better off to have just filed bankruptcy and not gone through all the debt settlement. Absolutely not. The lessons I learned in facing my debt and the joys I felt in making the settlements, the journey I went through in releasing the pain and suffering, all of that made the debt-settlement process far more worthwhile, for me, than to have just filed bankruptcy. I always knew that, like anyone, I would still need to find work and income to sustain my future even after successfully negotiating settlements on my debt.

Then, hallelujah, I got a job! A film script that I had written three years earlier was being made, and I was hired to be on set during the shoot for production revisions. To cap off the joy of work and a movie getting made, it was being filmed in Europe. I was thrilled to get a little time away (two months!), to be working again and to be receiving a paycheck.

I felt almost awkward mailing the deposits to my bank, as if some arcane rule saying my account was closed because I hadn't made a deposit for so long would apply. I wasn't going to be destitute just yet, but I also wasn't completely done with this journey.

While in Europe, I wasn't checking my voicemail very often. A cellphone call home was $3.50 a minute, and I hadn't yet discovered Skype-to-Phone. A couple of weeks into the trip, I checked my messages to hear a slew of collection calls. I realized that six months had passed on each account since I stopped making payments and that they had both gone into charge off. These were the new collection agencies calling me to see if I was going to be one of those files they could convert on.

Though I had kept up a policy of returning calls at least once a week during the settlement of all my other cards, because I was in Europe, I did not return these. I didn't want to get dragged into a half-hour conversation about my overdue balances at $3.50 a minute.

I did not call them back until I returned home in July 2009. Fortunately, now I could start settlement negotiations again. My two outstanding card balances had increased with interest in the time I hadn't been making payments. White Bank went up from $12,500 to $15,000 and Green Bank from $17,500 to $22,500.

I explained my entire story to them, that I had settled out all my other debts and that I had just earned my first income in two years. I had earned $16,000 and said to them both, "The first call I'm making is to you to see if we can settle out these debts."

I told them that I had set aside $5,000 to settle and would send it to the first one who accepted the offer. They both refused. I wasn't surprised. These were new collection agents and both were opening in the 85-percent range. But as expected, they were negotiating.

I was actually feeling pretty good about things in the summer of 2009. I had a little money in the bank and was back in negotiations to settle my last two credit cards. I finally closed a deal with a U.S. distributor to release *Uncross the Stars* on DVD, and it was slated to hit the streets in September.

In August 2009, I held my first, live Do-It-Yourself Bailout seminar in Los Angeles and had the pleasure of meeting many of my readers face to face. The seminar allowed me to add a lot of material that I'd learned after writing the book. I had the seminar videotaped and made into a DVD that people could use in conjunction with the book to overcome their debt and fears. As it turned out, I was as much a participant in that seminar as a leader because I actually heard of a few new types of offers that were being made that had not been available when I was settling my first five cards. That information would be very helpful to me when, a few weeks later, White Bank and Green Bank started coming down on their offers.

White Bank said it would take a 50-percent settlement, cutting my balance from $15,000 to $7,500. Rather than having to pay the entire $7,500 settlement upfront, or even over three to four monthly payments, I could pay half of the settlement, $3,750, and then $100 a month for three years to settle the rest, at no interest! I actually found myself thinking, "That's a pretty good deal."

However, I didn't want to pay $7,500 on that card; nor did I want to go back on a payment plan, even with such low payments, because I had no idea what my future income would be. I was also pretty sure the deal would come with some penalties if I missed a payment, just as settlement agreements that allow for a few payments are voided if one is missed. I repeated that I would send them the $5,000 I had set aside as full settlement. Again, they refused.

Too bad for them. Not long after, Green Bank called out of the blue to ask if I would still make the $5,000 settlement. I said I would. They didn't even negotiate, but there was a twist (there's always a twist, right?). They wanted the payment immediately, that very morning. They didn't want to wait a day to receive a cashier's check by overnight courier (which is how I had sent in most of my previous settlement payments). They wanted to do a payment by phone. The only other time I had considered doing a payment by phone was with Yellow Bank, more than a year earlier, which is the bank that tried to collect on the balance after the settlement. I had paid them by wire transfer, but at least had a paper receipt from the bank showing that the payment had been made. A payment by phone would have no paper receipt, and I was really pretty concerned about giving out my saving's account number, bank-routing number, and other such information over the phone.

I really balked at this. I told them I could send them the payment by cashier's check overnight. I told them I could do a wire transfer the next morning (it was past 2 p.m., the cutoff time for wire transfers in Los Angeles). They refused it all. They said that the account was going into charge off the next day, and their motivation for taking the low settlement offer (it was only 22 percent) was to have it on their books instead of going to another collection agent's books.

I agreed to do the payment by phone, but not before getting the settlement agreement in writing, of course (Document 11, below).

RECOVERY SYSTEMS

Creditor: SAVINGS BANK
Account:
URS ID:
October 30, 2009   Amount Due as of October 30, 2009: $22,701.18

Kenneth Golde   Recovery Systems, LP

Los Angeles, CA

Please detach at perforation and return with your payment

SETTLEMENT OFFER!!!

Our client has agreed to accept 1 payment(s) totaling $5,000.00 as settlement in full for monies owing on your account. Please make your check or money order payable to our client.

Please note, failure to make payments as scheduled will cancel the agreement and result in the entire balance becoming due.

Notice: The internal revenue service may require financial institutions to file Form 1099-C (Cancellation of Debt) to report the discharge of indebtedness of $600.00 or more.

You understand that this settlement does not completely resolve the loss that was sustained by   and certain restrictions may still be applied to any present or future business relationships with this or other   companies.

This communication is from a debt collector. We are required to inform you that this is an attempt to collect a debt, and any information obtained will be used for this purpose.

Sincerely,

Document 11: Green Bank settlement agreement

Here it is, showing a $5,000 settlement on a balance of $22,701.

The payment by phone turned out to be no problem. In fact, they sent me a "Final Release" acknowledging the payment so I even had the paper trail I wanted. There were no repercussions, and I had just made a $5,000 settlement on a $22,700 balance.

Way back in the summer of 2008, about fifteen months earlier, I had a dream of being debt free. Now I had reduced my credit card debt from $219,500 (my original $212,000 plus the added interest on Green and White Bank) to just $15,000 (White Bank). However, my savings were dwindling again. The money I had earned in May and June, I had now lived on for six months and spent a good portion settling this card.

In September 2009, *Uncross the Stars* was finally released on DVD in the United States, fulfilling my commitment to Gabe to see the film in distribution and available for the public to enjoy. We received some really glowing reviews, and I know Gabe would have been proud. You can find the *Uncross the Stars* DVD on Amazon.com or our website, http://www.UncrosstheStarsMovie.com, and on Netflix. Though sales were slow and no money came in, creatively I felt, for the first time in about four years, that I was ready to start thinking about what my next movie would be.

I looked at the specifics of my career as a filmmaker. *Uncross the Stars*, a drama, had taken me more than a decade to finance and finally get into production. In contrast, my first feature film, *The Job*, a thriller, was written, financed, cast with Daryl Hannah and shot all in the same year (2002). I didn't want to wait another ten years before directing my next film, so I decided to write a thriller. Moreover, I wanted to make a film that I could get financed quickly and shoot easily. So I set out to create a movie with few production complications, but high-value entertainment.

I wrote a story that could be shot all in one house with limited camera equipment and natural lighting. With no location rentals, no company moves, no load-ins, no exteriors, no big equipment, a small cast, and a solid, scary thriller, I felt I could quickly raise three to four hundred thousand dollars and be making the film by spring.

Just before Christmas, I showed the script to my agent and managers, and after the New Year, they came back with great response. They loved it in a way they'd never loved anything I'd written. My agent said, "I have no notes." Unheard of. Everyone was excited to "do something" with the script. At the time, I still thought that meant raising a few hundred grand to shoot it.

We waited about a month. Then one Tuesday morning in February 2010, my agent "slipped" the script to four producers, meaning we weren't going out to the whole town with it as a traditional script sale might go. We were just testing the waters.

The waters heated up quickly. Within a few hours, the script had spread across Hollywood. It showed up on Internet "tracking boards" where development executives talk about hot scripts. Suddenly, dozens of producers were calling in asking to read it. By Wednesday, we were selecting which producers would be able to show it to which studios, all rather amazed that this tiny little script was getting attention from such big players.

By Friday afternoon, the script had sold. I was euphoric. Not only had I accomplished the dream of my twenty years in the entertainment business, to sell a script to a major studio producer, but I felt, finally, the complete turnaround from where I was just two years earlier. I had gone from being nearly a quarter of a million dollars in debt and miserable, to settling out nearly all of my debt and now setting my career as a screenwriter on fire.

Among countless lessons, many of which I discuss in this

book, I attribute the turnaround primarily to one thing: positive thought. From the day I decided that I would live my life fully without allowing my debt to define me, I redirected my future and was now reaping the rewards.

The script sale also relieved some financial pressure. While it didn't make me rich, it wasn't "life changing" money, it allowed me some breathing room. It also allowed me to settle out my last credit card.

I called White Bank. My account balance had increased to $17,800 with added interest over the past months. Their last offer was $7,500 and with the increased balance, I was expecting them to offer $8,000 to $9000 and that I would have to negotiate a little. You'll recall that my last offer was $5,000, and I was prepared to pay $7,000.

In my seminar DVD, I talk about the power of fixing the number in your mind that you are prepared to settle for and how often it will turn out just that way. Here was more proof. They offered $7,100. I took it without countering. While the percentage was a little higher than my other cards, about 40 percent, I've often counseled people that a settlement is not always about the percentage. You should look at the actual dollar figures and determine what is right for you. After three years, saving another grand was not worth spending another day in debt. Interestingly, the $7,100 settlement was still less than their previous offer of $7,500, even though the balance had increased from $15,000 to $18,000. In essence, the added interest had no bearing on the settlement, and I still settled for less money by waiting an additional six months. And now, I was 100 percent credit-card debt free!

KENNETH GOLDE

LOS ANGELES, CA

| Forward Payment To:
CREDIT & COLLECTION CORP.

Detach and Return Top Portion With Payment

Client:
Account #:   Amount: $17,794.28

April 22, 2010

Dear KENNETH GOLD

This letter shall serve to confirm that   Credit & Collection Corp. is the duly authorized agent acting on behalf of
         We are prepared to accept the sum of **$7,117.71** as final settlement of this account.
Conditions of this settlement are as follows:

1) The payment of **$7,117.71** must be paid to   Credit & Collection Corp. on or before 3pm before
   April 26, 2010
2) Payment may not be returned by a financial institution for any reason.

If the conditions of this settlement are not met, this settlement will be considered null and void. If the terms of this
settlement are met your Credit Bureau will be updated accordingly. A release letter will subsequently be provided.

Note: The internal Revenue Service requires the Creditor to provide it with information about amounts of $600.00 or
more that are discharged as a result of a cancellation of debt If the amount the Creditor will discharge when the final
payment of your settlement is received is $600.00 or more, the Creditor will be required to notify the IRS of the
discharged amount. You will receive a copy of the form 1099C that will be filed with the IRS.

Yours truly,

Document 12: White Bank settlement agreement

My final credit card settlements looked like this:

Bank	Debt	Settlement	Savings
Yellow Bank	$76,000	$25,000	$51,000
Red Bank	$24,000	$9,300	$14,700
Blue Bank	$21,000	$7,400	$13,600
Green Bank	$22,700*	$5,000	$17,700
White Bank	$17,800*	$7,100	$10,700
Brown Bank 1	$22,000	$10,000	$12,000
Brown Bank 2	$39,000	$15,000	$24,000
Total	**$222,500***	**$78,800 (35%)**	**$143,700**

* Green Bank was originally $17,500 but increased $5,200 in additional interest during the months I wasn't paying on the card. White Bank was originally $12,500 and increased $5300 with added interest. My original debt was $212,000 and increased a total of $10,000 with added interest during the 12 to 18-month periods I was not making payments on those two cards.

As with the script sale, I attribute my being 100 percent debt free to setting a positive vision and intent, letting go of the emotions that would hinder or prevent me from living into that intent, being patient and staying committed to my vision no matter what setbacks (financial or emotional) threatened to dissuade me.

Of course, the setbacks continued.

WORKSHEET: "MANY SUCCESSES"

This time, just a few of my favorite quotes:

"Success is the ability to move from failure to failure without loss of enthusiasm."

— Winston Churchill

"Whatever you can do, or dream you can do, begin it. Boldness has genius, power and magic in it. Begin it. Begin it now."

— Johann Goethe

"Don't worry. Be happy."

— Bobby McFerrin

Chapter 8

FORECLOSURE

ABOUT ONE WEEK AFTER SETTLING my last credit card, my house was sold at a foreclosure auction.

The problems with my home mortgage had begun long before my credit-card debt crisis. In fact, my mortgage was a cog in the machinery that helped contribute to the 2008 financial crisis. In 2005, I had purchased my home with an adjustable-rate mortgage. Oh, I put in a down payment, a sizable one. And at the interest rate that my loan started at, I remained current on my mortgage without problem for some time. Then interest rates started to rise. From 2005 to 2007, it seemed as if the prime rate went up a quarter of a percent, which equated to about $100 on my mortgage, every month. Over two years, I watched my monthly payment increase by more than $2,000, nearly doubling.

Nevertheless, I remained current through 2007 when my credit-card debt crisis began and nearly all of 2008 while I was settling most of my credit accounts. However, by November 2008, I was extremely cash poor. I had resorted to making the minimum, "negative amortization" payment that added to my principal balance each month, and finally called my lender to tell them that I was in financial difficulty and to ask what help they could offer. The person on the phone looked up my account and saw that I was current in my payments.

He said, "We do have a department that can offer assistance to homeowners in distress, but we cannot connect you to them while you are current on your mortgage."

Given my experience with the credit cards, I was not surprised, though I couldn't resist saying, "Are you telling me not to pay my mortgage?"

He answered, "No, I'm telling you that we have a department that can help you, but I cannot transfer you to them while you are current on your mortgage."

The British would call that "cheeky."

When I missed my second payment in December, I received a call telling me that I now "qualified" for their homeowner-assistance program. Isn't it curious how I did not qualify for assistance when I called to ask for it, but once I'd stopped making my mortgage payment, I was a candidate for the help I needed? I had to fill out a form declaring much of my financial situation and would then have to wait for a response.

As we ended the call, the man on the phone read what was clearly a prepared script. "I'm required to tell you that as long as you are behind in your payments, you could continue to receive calls, interest and penalties will accrue on your account, and at the end of the month, any delinquencies in your account could be reported to the credit bureaus and reflect negatively on your credit score."

Six months later, in April 2009, I received a loan-modification offer. I had been hoping for two primary results from a loan modification: reduction of my principal balance to the current market value of my home (about a $200,000 reduction) and changing my adjustable-rate mortgage to a fixed rate, then about 3.5 percent. Those two things would have brought my mortgage payment down by more than half, back to the level it was at when I first bought the home four years earlier.

The loan offer I received did not meet either of those goals. They offered me a 2-percent fixed rate for five years with no principal reduction. After the five years, my mortgage would balloon to the current market interest rates. While this would reduce my monthly payment and stop adding to my principal, I saw the offer as a way for the bank (when looked at across the mortgage crisis of the entire country) to simply stem the flow of foreclosures for the moment while setting us up for another crash when everyone's new balloon payments kicked in. I opposed this solution both in theory and in personal practice as I didn't want to be back in the same boat five years on.

Having just been so successful in negotiating all of my credit-card debt, I thought I could negotiate my loan-modification offer, also. I countered with a request for principal reduction and a permanent, fixed mortgage rate. The person on the phone said I was "not allowed" to make a counterproposal, those were her words, "not allowed." She indicated that I should have been thankful to receive any offer at all, which I immediately recognized as a play on my emotions intended to persuade me to take the offer. I did not accept, believing I could still get someone to negotiate with me. I was wrong.

When I called a few weeks later to inquire about the status, I was told that offer had expired and that I would have to start from scratch and reapply for a new loan modification, which I did in May 2009.

About a month later, while I was in Europe working on the film I had written, I received a letter informing me that my home was going into foreclosure. Unfortunately, I didn't see the letter until I returned in July.

I immediately called the bank to see what I could do. I explained to them that I had an application in for a loan modification. Apparently, the loan-modification department and the foreclosure department didn't communicate much. They told me that I would move toward foreclosure unless I started making payments again, regardless of my loan-modification application. This was contrary to what they told me months earlier, that I needed to not be making payments to apply for a modification.

In any case, I couldn't afford to go back to my full monthly payment. They offered to put me on a "forbearance plan" that allowed me to make a greatly reduced monthly payment (about 30 percent of my regular monthly payment), which would put a hold on the foreclosure proceedings while I waited to see if my second modification application was approved.

While waiting, I decided that I would take the 2 percent for five years when it was offered again. I'd only denied it out of the spirit of negotiations. When I learned that a home loan could not be negotiated in the same way a credit-card balance could, it seemed that reducing my payments to an affordable rate for five years would be a benefit, allowing me to keep my home while looking for work, especially now that I wasn't dealing with the credit-card debt anymore.

In November 2009, the second modification was denied. So much for Plan A. Oddly, it was denied on the basis that I didn't have enough income. I got a chuckle out of this, given that I had zero income for two years when my first application resulted in a modification offer, and now that I'd made some money over the summer, it wasn't enough to qualify for an offer. No one ever gave me a suitable explanation for that logic. I was told I could apply again and expected that I could just continue my forbearance plan at the reduced rate to stave off foreclosure proceedings.

That, too, was denied. No more forbearance plan. The only way for me to stop foreclosure proceedings now was to make a full payment on the entire past due balance on my mortgage, about $60,000. I didn't have a tenth of that in savings.

In March 2010, I received the Notice of a Deed of Trust Sale. On April 12, three years after going into debt of more than $200,000 and one week after settling my last credit card, my home was sold at public auction.

Like many homeowners, or as the case may be, former homeowners, I didn't know what to do in this situation. When would I have to move out? Would I be evicted? Could I stay and rent back from the bank? I didn't have to wait long for answers. Within three days of the sale, a real-estate agent representing the bank arrived at my house to offer me "cash for keys," meaning they would give me $1,000 if I would stipulate a move-out date and be gone by that date. My understanding was that the reason they made such an offer was to save themselves the cost of eviction proceedings. I asked to have a clause written into the cash-for-keys agreement stipulating that they would not pursue eviction proceedings against me unless I did not move out on the agreed-upon date. They refused to alter the agreement, though I was told verbally on the phone that they would not file for eviction unless the move-out date passed and I was still in the house. Contrary to my own advice on settlement agreements, I signed even though I was not happy with the language. We agreed on June 10, giving me two months to find a new place to live.

Two weeks later, I received an Unlawful Detainer complaint, the legal step required for the bank to get a judgment against me that would allow them to file for eviction. So much for the verbal guarantee. All of those emotions I had fought so hard to conquer came rushing back in. I wasn't upset about the foreclosure itself—I had long ago separated any identity attachment I might have once had to the term "foreclosure." I felt no stigma or shame in returning my home to the bank. Purchasing a home is a business transaction, just like taking out a credit-card loan. And while credit-card companies have every right to pursue their interests, so do home lenders. I had chosen to make my film, which put me into debt. I had chosen to use the available money I had, when I had it, to put toward credit-card settlements instead of my mortgage. I was okay with the bank taking the action they needed to protect their investment.

I was not okay with them lying to me. Now I had to hire an attorney to file a response to the complaint, which cost much of the $1,000 I would receive from them for moving out. And I had to go to court. I had to appear as the defendant in the Unlawful Detainer suit. And you know what? I'm glad I did. Guess what I learned?

There was a settlement opportunity. The moment court was in session, the judge spent a half-hour telling everyone present that he recommended all parties go into the hall and attempt to settle their lawsuits before pleading their cases before him.

In my case, no settlement was necessary. My attorney explained to the opposing attorney that there was a stipulated move-out agreement, of which he was unaware. In the end, we all agreed that if I moved out on the tenth of June, the suit would be dismissed. I did, and it was. While I felt the entire suit could have been avoided and saved me money and time, it was worth the experience of going to court to learn that it wasn't that bad. My heart wasn't pounding standing there as a defendant in a lawsuit. There was no fear or anxiety, no sweat on my brow, no stress. It was business. I was fine with it. That was a major emotional victory for me over my previous identity attachment to finance or foreclosure.

Ultimately, it was a financial victory as well. My home was worth about 60 percent of what I'd paid for it, and the mortgage was costing me twice as much as it would cost to rent the same house at current market value. In giving it back to the bank, I walked away from another $200,000 to $300,000 in debt (the upside-down portion of the mortgage) and was able to rent a nicer home in a better neighborhood for less money. A win all around.

I also learned something about "judicial" versus "nonjudicial" foreclosures. This information may help some of you who are in a foreclosure situation, though I can only attest that what I learned is true in California. It may vary in other states. Evidently, there are two types of foreclosures in California, "judicial," which means the bank files a lawsuit in court for the foreclosure, and "nonjudicial," which is a Deed of Trust sale at auction not put through the court. While the homeowner may be liable for the deficiency in a judicial sale, meaning the bank could pursue the homeowner for the difference between the sale amount and the loan amount, in a Deed of Trust sale, the homeowner is freed from any deficiency liability, as I was. Also, recent laws (passed during the financial crisis of the past couple of years, though I cannot cite them) have also eliminated, for the time being, any 1099 tax burden on the forgiven deficiency in a foreclosure sale. Thus, I was completely freed from any debt or tax burden after the sale.

Now I was truly debt free. No credit-card debt. No auto debt. No home loan. No tax liability.

You may be wondering, not just at this moment but throughout reading this book, how all of these experiences affected my credit score. Well, I was, too. I've checked it twice in the past few years. Once, in the fall of 2008, after missing my monthly payments on seven credit cards for a year and a half and negotiating settlements on the first five, and missing several mortgage payments, but not yet having my house foreclosed, it was 606. Six months later, after settling my last two credit cards (the final $30,000), having $143,000 in debt written off, not making payments on my home mortgage for about eighteen months and having my home foreclosed, it was 593. Certainly not the 780 or so I started with, but not horrible. Not life shattering. Not as bad as it would be to still be making $3,600 a month in interest payments on well more than $200,000 in credit-card debt and paying $4,000 a month on a home that was $200,000 upside down in its loan to value ratio.

Generally, I have found that just as people attach a lot of emotion and identity to their finances, they do the same to their credit score. I had a friend once tell me that she didn't want to buy a house (actually, she *did* want to buy a house, but convinced herself that she didn't) because, as her ill-logic went, "If I ever lose my job and have to miss a mortgage payment, my credit score might go down." I found it fascinating. She had entirely missed the point that, having already *bought* a house (in her hypothetical), it wouldn't matter that her credit score fell a little bit if she'd ever lost her job and missed a payment. But more than that, she was going to deny herself the pleasure of home ownership out of the *fear* that the potential for missing a payment might lower her credit score. Her credit score was more important to her than the house she would use it to buy. Why? Because she had vested personal identity, her personal sense of self-worth, in her credit score. Anyone else guilty of that?

This is something I say to many of my readers and discuss in detail in my seminar DVD, "Your Credit Score is not the *end-all.*" It is a tool that lenders use to determine whether they will lend to you and if they do, at what terms. Yes, sometimes, it is also a tool that landlords use to determine whether they will rent to you and occasionally, that employers throw into the mix of hiring considerations. However, your credit score *does not* define who you are as a person. Anything emotional that you are attaching to your credit score is social programming reinforced by television commercials for credit-monitoring services.

If you are lightly in credit-card debt and looking to buy a home, then debt settlement is not for you. If you own your home, or rent but are not looking to buy soon nor take out any large loans in the near future, and your are carrying burdensome credit-card debt that is eating into your income in a way that your ability to provide for yourself or your family is suffering, then the only piece of actual advice that I will give in this book is this: Do not allow the emotional fear of having a lower credit score stop you from exploring all your options. A low credit score does not make you a bad person any more than a high credit score makes someone a good person. It just makes them someone with access to lots of credit.

In the last two years since settling all of my credit-card debt and having my home foreclosed, I was able to rent a nice house in a nice neighborhood, advance my career far beyond where it had previously been, and am now more than a year into a new relationship. Not one of the people involved ever asked for my credit score.

My final conclusion is this: I wouldn't trade the last five years for anything. The debt took me through an incredible journey of life and emotion and lessons about finance and identity. I've been interviewed on TV and radio, held a live debt-settlement seminar, and become a public speaker on debt settlement. I have been able to help others free themselves from the emotional burden of debt. I believe that my positive attitude led to selling my first "big" screenplay, and that has opened up many new opportunities for me as a screenwriter and filmmaker, including my first studio-level writing assignment and several films now financed and on their way to production. I have a new love in my life, the woman who I am going to marry and finally fulfill our mutual dream of having a family. I have fully lived and engaged in life in the past few years, with all of its ups and downs, expectations, disappointments, failures and successes, and am happier for and better for the experience.

My only regret is that I lost Gabe. I wish he could have seen the movie. In the end, this has all been for him.

Love you, Gabe.

Chapter 9

THE DEBT DOUBLE STANDARD
(MORALITY VS. LEGALITY)

D URING THE EVENTS THAT I describe in the previous chapters, from the very beginning when I was considering filing bankruptcy and through my experiences of debt settlement and home foreclosure, I turned to others I know who have gone through financial troubles, even bankruptcy, and gathered their experiences and opinions on the process. I found that many of them had already discovered the "debt as a commodity" concept that I encountered, and they showed me another nuance, one so subtle I was surprised, even shocked, to realize its truth.

When you hear the word "bankruptcy" and apply it to yourself, as in "I am going to file bankruptcy," how does that make you feel? When I first faced it, I felt fear, shame, anxiety, and a sense of failure. A brief survey of people I have met who share my situation, or one similar to it, has shown that such feelings are common among individuals in financial crisis. Contrarily, my friends in the business world describe a significantly different attitude toward bankruptcy. One attorney friend called bankruptcy a "strategy." It was pointed out to me that, in business, CEOs are not made to feel "wrong" or "bad" when revenue takes a downturn and they cannot pay off their business loans, even tens or hundreds of millions of dollars. They file bankruptcy, restructure their companies, write off large portions of their debt, work with banks to secure new credit, and open their doors again. These CEOs are often respected, if not heralded for coming through the hard times "successfully," even though they defaulted on millions of dollars in loans. Many such executives become highly paid "consultants" on the subject of negotiating out of debt.

Does that seem to you to be the general attitude extended toward individuals who file bankruptcy? Not to me it doesn't. We are told that our credit will be tarnished. It is certainly not something that the average person would bring up at a dinner party or on a date. Many people hide their dire financial situations from their friends, family, even their spouses. I believe that individuals have been conditioned, subtly to be sure, through a consistent "handing down" of a different set of standards between parents and children than are handed down from CEOs to their successors.

It appears there is a double standard between looking at finance on the basis of "legality" versus the basis of "morality." Individuals seem to be held to a moral standard, the label that you are a "bad" person who somehow "failed" if you cannot pay off your debts. Business operates on the basis of legality. If a business in the United States wants to do something that is currently not legal under whatever provisions apply, they will lobby the local, state, or federal legislature to modify, amend, or create a law that makes what they want to do legal. Why do you think there are so many lobbyists in Washington? They are there to push legislation that will benefit their clients. If a particular state law prohibits a brewer from selling beer in excess of 3 percent alcohol, and the brewer wants to sell beer with 5 percent alcohol, they don't peddle bootleg beer. They lobby their legislature to increase the legal limit of alcohol by volume. If they are successful, then they sell the higher-potency beer.

Quite often, it is difficult to distinguish when a new law is in the public interest and when it is in the interest of private business. It was certainly in the public interest when it became law in California that every driver have auto insurance. It also greatly benefited the auto-insurance industry by establishing a legal requirement that every California driver buy their product.

Taking this concept directly to the banking industry, each state is allowed to set its own maximum interest rates that a bank can charge on a loan. To exceed this limit would be considered *usury*,[9] the term applied to charging excessive interest. There is also a federal law (federal laws supersede state laws) stating that any bank labeling itself with the word "national" or "N.A." is exempt from its home state's usury limit and can, by federal statute, charge interest up to twice as high as the home state's. (I'd always wondered at the meaning behind Chase Bank USA, N.A., or Wells Fargo Bank, N.A.) At some point, someone, whether a lobbyist, a lawyer, a bank or consortium of banks, or some other business interest, appealed to Congress to pass this law allowing banks to charge higher interest rates and make more money. I do not contend that this is wrong. I only point it out as a particular instance, related to banking, where a private company put forth the notion of changing a law so that they could increase their profits, and Congress approved. Within this construct, there is no moral argument for what "excessive" interest is, only the legal limit.

Similarly, the Bankruptcy Abuse Prevention Act of 2005,

---

[9] Try *www.bankrate.com/brm/news/cc/20020320a.asp* or *http://www.usurylaw. com*.

which made it more difficult for consumers to wipe away debt, was put forth by banking interests that felt a change in that law would allow them to increase their profits. Responsively, consumer groups lobbied for some changes to bank and lending laws that would favor the borrowers, and in Februray 2010, the Credit Card Accountability, Responsibility and Disclosure Act of 2009 became law, delineating new practices for lenders to follow. Again, I am not judging either law, or the people behind them, as right or wrong. Both sides were simply seeking legal support for their best interests.

I find an interesting detail in here. The Credit CARD Act of 2009 was touted as having many "benefits" for consumers,[10] and they are all, at a glance, seemingly positive, if one were to judge them on the basis of positive or negative. So why is that we, as individuals, are taught to think negatively of the provisions contained in the bankruptcy laws that also work to our benefit, and for that matter, the ability to allow one's house to be foreclosed and be relieved of the loan obligations and the ability to negotiate settlements on credit-card debt? Why do we feel that it is all right to take refuge behind some laws that work in our favor, yet judge ourselves, or have others judge us, for taking advantage of other laws that benefit us?

My argument is that if banks are allowed to lobby legislatures to pass laws that favor their business and then pursue their rights under such laws, isn't it equally legitimate that individuals should be free to pursue all the laws that favor them, also without judgment? Why is it that if business, es-

---

[10] You'll find a good summary of the 2009 Credit CARD Act's major provisions at: *http://www.bankrate.com/finance/credit-cards/8-major-benefits-of-new-credit-card-law-1.aspx*

pecially large business, is allowed to operate on the level of legality, that individuals are still expected to operate on morality? Why should a collection agent bring my integrity into question in an attempt to make me feel "wrong" because I am not making credit-card payments? It's legal. I don't question their integrity when it comes to purchasing my debt at ten cents on the dollar and then pursuing me to collect, despite my belief that I could make a pretty good *moral* argument that doing so is unscrupulous, because it, too, is *legal.*

What I hope to accomplish here is a shift in the public thinking about debt. We are encouraged to accumulate debt at every stage in life. Student loans, car loans, home loans, gas-station cards, department-store cards, credit cards, and so on. In a world that encourages so much debt, the building of debt is to be expected. In the building of such debt, the defaulting of debt is to be expected. It is a risk that banks take on in the business of lending money, just like any other business takes on risks.

With this realization and others I have described, I have become resolved not to suffer emotionally either because I got into serious debt or because I was able to get out of it through negotiating settlements. I will not allow my financial situation to define my self-worth. Negotiating through debt is a business transaction, and I treat it as such, legally, and without personal recrimination.

Remember my definition of **Debt-ication?**

"A feeling of gratitude to my state of owing money. A commitment to the purpose of self-growth and discovery through the journey of paying off my debts, monetary and personal."

Yes, I have eliminated my credit-card debt, but that is not self-growth. The growth was the process I went through emotionally that allowed me to successfully negotiate my debt. I have succeeded in separating emotionality from finance. I am not attaching my self-worth to my bank account nor am I allowing the debt double standard to affect my identity. I feel that my newfound independence from emotion in the realm of money will lead to greater financial success in my future, and greater happiness, not simply because of the money I earn, but because I will not torture myself over its comings and goings. Perhaps that is true financial freedom.

Chapter 10

AN ANECDOTE

M Y NEW YEAR'S RESOLUTION FOR 2007 was that for my fortieth birthday in May, I would either be in production
on a film or at the Cannes Film Festival in France, to which
I had never been. I was lucky enough to be on set shooting
Uncross the Stars. The next May, just after I had instructed
my attorney to start pursuing settlements with my credit-card
companies, I was turning forty-one, and I wanted to make
the Cannes dream come true.

I'll admit to feeling a conflicting sense of guilt, being on
the verge of bankruptcy and considering a trip to the south
of France. I had stopped making my credit-card payments in
order to extend my available cash as long as possible, giving
me the best opportunity to sell the film and pay off my debt
prior to going bankrupt. Of course, it wouldn't be a vacation.
I'm not saying it wouldn't be fun, but it was a business trip.
My film was showing at the film market there, and I had an
opportunity to meet an Italian producer who had expressed
an interest in hiring me to direct a film, which, if it happened, would produce an income. I couldn't afford a flight,
which was well more than $1,500 at the time. Though per-
haps the one advantage of running a movie through credit
cards is the accumulation of frequent-flyer miles. I set myself
a rather low budget (ridiculously low given the exchange rate

that summer) and decided that if I could get a free flight using award miles and a cheap room, I could make it work.

Also, going to Cannes would be a direct expression of my new context: to live my life fully and with dignity while carrying my debt, rather than crawl into a debt hole and not fully engage in living. Soon, I would get to see firsthand, as this anecdote will tell, just how important that fresh context would be. In short, it made the trip.

I was able to book a flight to Cannes with miles, but it wasn't pretty.

Los Angeles-London, London-Frankfurt, Frankfurt-Nice. And that included a nearly five-hour stopover in Frankfurt. The London-Frankfurt leg arrived at 12:20 p.m. There was a 1:10 p.m. flight to Nice, but they wouldn't book me on it because they required a minimum one-hour gap for it to be a valid connecting flight. The next flight out was at nearly 5 p.m. I wanted to sit in the Frankfurt airport for a whole afternoon on my way to Cannes about as much as I wanted to be more than $200,000 in debt. So I stuffed all of my things into one carry-on bag, checked no luggage, and made the entire trip with the solitary purpose of making the 1:10 flight out of Frankfurt on standby. At the time, I didn't even know if there would be seats available.

The first leg was easy going. I carried on my bag in L.A. and settled in for ten and a half hours to London. It was upon arriving at Heathrow that my choice started to be a burden. The fairly new Terminal 5 at Heathrow is the size of a small city. Getting off the plane, we didn't walk up a jetway into the terminal, but down a staircase to the tarmac where they loaded us onto a bus and drove us fifteen minutes through the underground baggage-sorting area to the very front of the airport. I then went through security and passport control and had to walk nearly a mile back to the gate for my next plane. All with my luggage.

The flight to Frankfurt was delayed a half-hour, and instead of arriving at 12:20 p.m., we landed at 12:45 p.m. I was certain now that I would never make the 1:10 p.m. flight, but as we pulled up to the gate, I became momentarily hopeful that I could walk up the jetway, go one or two gates over, and still get on. But no. Apparently, they do things all over the EU much the same. The staircase. The tarmac. The bus. All with my luggage. To the front of the airport, through security and passport control. By the time I was in the terminal, it was 1:10 p.m., and with a sigh, I resigned myself to the four-hour wait until my scheduled flight to Nice. Then I caught sight of a monitor for departing flights and saw that the flight to Nice was delayed to 1:25 p.m. I started to run.

Frankfurt airport is not easy to negotiate. Different hallways for different passport holders, gates and terminals all scattered in different directions. It's huge. I ran at least another mile, up and down staircases with my bag. Finally, sweating through my shirt, I arrived at the gate. Miraculously, the plane was still there.

"For Nice?" the gate attendant asked me. I nodded yes and gave her my ticket and passport, quickly explaining my situation, that I was booked on the 4:45 flight, but wanted to go on this one. She scanned my ticket and said that I could take the flight, but there would be a 30-euro change fee. I reached in my wallet, happy to pay it, only to be told that they could not accept the fee at this gate. I would have to pay it at the check-in counter for the airline, all the way back at the front of the airport.

I moaned, exasperated. We both knew there was no way I was getting back there and back here again, though security and passport control, in the seconds they had before this flight took off. She apologized and suggested I check at the next gate over to see if they could take my payment.

So I ran to the next gate. And to the next. Same story each time. As I ran back to the original gate, nearly certain that the flight had left, the compound rubber wheels on my luggage had heated up so much in all the running that they both disintegrated, smearing a long streak of black grease on the linoleum floor, like a car skid, so that I was now dragging my bag with no wheels, sparks flying.

And it was this sight, this sweaty, haggard American with sparks flying off his bag, that returned to the gate for the flight to Nice. The gate attendant knew I hadn't paid my change fee. "Please," I begged, "please don't make me sit here for four hours when I could be in the south of France. I have a ticket for the flight. You have seats . . ."

She waved me through. I couldn't believe it. In Germany! As I hurried down the ramp, I saw that the plane door had already closed. They actually opened the plane door for me to get on. The flight attendant on board looked at my bag and said there were no overhead bins available and there was no time to check the bag underneath the plane. If I couldn't fit my bag under a seat, I'd have to get off and wait for the next flight. I'd never even tried to fit this bag under a plane seat before, and it was way overstuffed because I wanted to fit everything in one bag for the very purpose of getting on this flight.

I took the first seat I could find, row two, and kicked and stuffed that bag under the seat until it was a part of the plane. I sat, exhausted. The plane was backing away from the gate when the flight attendant returned. "I'm sorry, sir, this is a first-class seat, and you have a ticket for coach. You'll have to go back to your seat. You can leave your bag here." Though there seemed to be a certain silliness around following that strict rule at this point — the plane was taking off, no one else was going to sit in that seat, and it was only a forty-five-minute flight — I wasn't about to complain. I had left Los Angeles seventeen hours earlier intending to make this flight, and I was on it, the happiest one on it, I'm sure.

As I walked down the aisle — hair wet, white shirt soaked through to my skin — everyone was looking at me like I was certainly the reason their plane was taking off twenty minutes late. No matter.

My seat was in the very back row, in the middle. I plopped down, all sweaty, with a smile on my face, a smile so big that the man in the window seat said, "I've got to hear this story."

"Bill" turned out to be a great guy, a venture capitalist from Seattle. He was heading down to Monte Carlo for the Monaco Grand Prix Formula One race where his company had leased a 210-foot yacht to entertain European investors. We started talking movies and tech start-ups, and I told him the story I've just told you about making the flight, happy and enthusiastic about the entire adventure. As we were getting off the plane, he invited me to come to the yacht for the weekend. I accepted, of course, just needing to get over to Cannes first to see what was going on with my foreign-sales agent there.

I arrived in Cannes to a beautiful, sunny, cool afternoon. My room turned out to be only a ten-minute walk from the beach. The first thing I did was walk to the International Pavilion where all the sales companies set up their booths. I found my company and saw the poster for my film. I wished Gabe could have been there with me.

I spent several days connecting with old friends and making

new ones, meeting the Italian producer who was interested in having me direct his film, and working on the international sales of *Uncross the Stars.*

As the weekend of the Monaco Grand Prix approached, I decided to get more information on heading over to Monte Carlo.

I had never been to the south of France, and I had no idea what the geographical relationship was between Cannes and Monte Carlo. All I knew about how to get to Monaco was that Bill had said there was a helicopter that went from Nice to Monaco for 99 euros. I was naively hoping this would be 99 euros round trip. Silly of me. Of course, it was each way.

I called Bill to confirm that I was still invited. He said sure, he'd love to have me, but had a long story about how many of the arrangements on the boat had gone awry and though I was welcome to come visit, all of the rooms on the boat were filled, and I wouldn't be able to stay the night. I said, "No problem" and jumped on the Internet to find a room. I didn't have much hope for finding a room in Monte Carlo on Grand Prix weekend, but luckily, there was an opening. Two hundred and fifty euros for the night. (If you are wondering how I paid for it online, I did use a credit card. Remember, I'd kept two cards current for such situations.)

The summer I was in France, oil was selling in New York and London at a record high of nearly $140 a barrel, which meant the dollar was at a record low of about $1.70 to the euro. Because I had no credit, I brought cash (a mistake, I highly recommend using ATMs in world travel whenever possible as the ubiquitous "change" booths often charge very high commissions). I was paying 18-percent commission on my cash, which brought my effective exchange rate to nearly $2 to the euro.

So, what I originally hoped was going to be a $200 helicopter ride to Monte Carlo was now a $400 helicopter ride and a $500 hotel room. Hmm. That's a lot of money for a single night. Still, it sounded like a once-in-a-lifetime experience and an opportunity to pursue a friendship with a venture capitalist who was doing well enough to lease yachts for Grand Prix. Saving $900 didn't seem like the right move if I was going to pursue business possibilities and hold my context of continuing to live my life fully without letting the debt define my identity or affect my actions.

On Saturday morning, I woke up, prepared to go to Monte Carlo. I thought, it being Grand Prix weekend, that the helicopter might require a reservation so I called. Yes, there were seats available. I then said, "I just want to confirm that it is two hundred euros round trip."

You must imagine the answer coming from a sweet, young woman's voice in a French accent. Like Audrey Tautou speaking English. "No no no. It is Grand Prix. The cost is two hundred-fifty euros each way, five hundred euros round trip."

Gulp. That's $1,000 dollars plus the hotel room at $500. That's a really expensive day in Monte Carlo. At this point, the context of "keep living my life" was very challenging. Not yet ready to pull that trigger, I slumped down the stairs to the living room of the apartment where I was staying. My whole body must've really lost my context because the nice woman I was renting the room from asked me what was wrong. Isn't it interesting how much our physical form conveys of our mood?

I told her the story of the expensive helicopter flight, and she said, "But why don't you take the train?"

"There's a train?!"

I had no idea. Hadn't even thought of it. The train station, it turned out, was a five-minute walk from the room. I'd passed beneath it each time I'd walked to the beach. The train was easier to take than the helicopter would have been because it left directly from Cannes. The helicopter required a taxi ride to the Nice airport, then doing the whole airport thing.

And the best part: The train was seven euros. Moreover, on this particular Saturday, there was a strike on the French rail system. The train operators were working, but the ticket-window attendants and onboard controllers were not. I couldn't buy a ticket at the station, so I took a seat on the train expecting someone to come sell me one en route. No one ever did. I arrived in Monte Carlo forty-five minutes later — for free.

The first thing I noticed stepping out of the station was how loud it was. The cars that raced by on the main street that circled the harbor were so loud that many people were walking around with giant ear muffs, not the warm and fuzzy skiing kind, the hard-shell racetrack kind.

I met Bill on the dock, and we took a putt-putt boat out to the yacht. It was stunning. Three levels. A living room with a 50-inch plasma TV and a couch that sat twenty. A dining room with a table that sat thirty-six. A full-sized bar with premium drinks, beers, wines, and Champagnes. The bedrooms, about ten of them, had queen beds and full-sized bathrooms with shower-tubs. The Jacuzzi was fifteen feet across.

I spent the evening drinking seventy-five dollar a glass Champagne, eating lamb chops, filet mignon, and langostinos, kicking back on the rear deck of a yacht that stretched two-thirds the length of a football field, listening to a warm and beautiful jazz singer they'd flown in from South Africa. I looked up at the hillside of Monte Carlo thinking, "This is what it feels like to be on the verge of bankruptcy? Not too bad. Not too bad at all."

Context is everything. What I got in touch with was that the pity-pot guy from six months earlier who was complaining about his situation, feeling like a failure, doubtful and depressed, would never be sitting there. I was on that boat because I'd sat down next to Bill with a smile on my face, happy to be a sweaty, mangled mess after running through two airports. That context is what caused him to turn and start a conversation with me, to invite me to the boat. I am a firm, unyielding believer that whatever concrete situations life throws at us, we are in control of how we look at them and how we deal with them. Context.

So, with happy thoughts in my head and a matching smile on my face, Bill came over to ask if I was having a good time. I was indeed. "Great," he said, "'cause it's time to go."

He had told me that there were no beds on the boat for me, and I was not disappointed at all. I'd had a great day and a great evening and was happy to help him succeed around the boat and his guests. The putt-putt returned me to shore where thousands of people were still up and out at the bars and restaurants in the city.

It was 1:30 a.m. The last train back to Cannes had left at midnight, but I hadn't even thought of that since I had the room booked. I found my hotel, which was not far, and walked in, saying hello, giving my name, and claiming my room.

They looked at me like I was crazy. I took out the confirmation from the online site where I booked the room. "I have a reservation."

Again, a cute girl with the French accent. "No, you don't."

"I do, look. It charged my credit card."

I handed her my printed receipt.

She ripped it in half.

I guffawed.

"We saw your reservation come through," she told me. "It was a mistake. We refunded your money and sent you an email." (An email I never saw because I left my room so early in the morning.) "It is Grand Prix this weekend. We have been booked for two years." (Though she didn't actually say it, I felt certain she wanted to end it all with, "What were you thinking, you silly American?")

So I didn't have a room. I headed back into the street where, I estimate, about 10,000 people were walking around, passing out beers, chatting about the race, and socializing. I spent the entire night with them. At 6 a.m., I caught the first train back to Cannes, arriving at 7 a.m., exactly twenty-four hours after I'd left. I'd had no sleep, the experience of a lifetime, and the only money I'd spent was on the most expensive plate of 4 a.m. french fries I'd ever had. Twenty dollars.

I hope I can live as richly when I do have money.

Thank you for reading *The Do-It-Yourself Bailout*. I truly hope that your time was well spent. I am happy to have shared my experiences with you and wish that you, too, may find relief from your debt and the emotions that go with it.

Kenny Golde
Los Angeles, Calif.
May 2012

THE DO-IT-YOURSELF BAILOUT
SEMINAR DVD

Would you like to have more information on talking to collection agents, including actual scripts from collection calls?

Would you like to go deeper into the emotional and identity attachment we have to money and credit scores in order to release those attachments so that you are more empowered in your finances?

Would you like more tangible tools on how to calculate when debt settlement is right for you or how a lower credit score might affect your next home or car loan?

Would you like additional help in figuring out how to come up with the money needed to make debt-settlement payments even when you believe you can't afford them and more personal insights from Kenny on how to successfully settle your own credit-card debt?

Then watch *The Do-It-Yourself Bailout* SEMINAR DVD, a forty-five-minute, live recording, only $19.

To purchase and watch free clips visit: *http://www.Settle YourCreditCards.com*

TO CONTACT THE AUTHOR

For more information on his films and books, please visit:
http://www.KennyGolde.com

For press, public appearances, and speaking engagements,
email Kenny at:
kgolde@roadrunner.com